Home

THREE
HOUSES

Home

THREE
HOUSES

ANNETTE
GOGGIN

Published by Redemption Press, PO Box 427, Enumclaw, WA 98022

Toll Free (844) 2REDEEM (273-3336)

Redemption Press is honored to present this title in partnership with the author. The views expressed or implied in this work are those of the author. Redemption Press provides our imprint seal representing design excellence, creative content, and high quality production.

Cover design by Brittany Osborn.

Grateful acknowledgment to Gwen Mathis for the photograph on page 24.

Stock Photos by:
© Can Stock Photo Inc. / littleny
© Can Stock Photo Inc. / THP
© kjpargeter / Freepik

All Scriptures are taken from the New King James Version, © 1979, 1980, 1982 by Thomas Nelson, Inc., Publishers. Used by permission.

ISBN: 978-1-68314-170-9

978-1-68314-171-6 ePub

978-1-68314-172-3 Mobi

Library of Congress Catalog Card Number: 2016957812

SCHOOLHOUSE

Thank you to Shirley Carmony, my eleventh-grade English teacher, colleague, mentor, and friend, both in and out of the schoolhouse for over thirty years. We said, "That's going in the book!" for years, and I wrote the first story in your condominium.

Thank you to my colleagues, especially those who offered a plethora of wisdom in my early days. I needed it.

Thank you to my students, both past and present. I have loved teaching you and knowing you.

CHURCH HOUSE

Thank you to my parents and family for making the church my second home and for pointing me to Christ.

Thank you to the wonderful church folk who put up with me as a PK, prayed for me over the years, and helped me raise good kids. I needed you the whole time.

FARMHOUSE

Thank you to Christina and Gus for gracing the farmhouse. We miss you at home but are proud of you where you are.

Thank you to Mark, my editor and best friend. I'm so glad I get to share a farmhouse and a lifetime with you.

"Oh, taste and see that the Lord is good; blessed is the man who trusts in Him" (Ps. 34:8).

TABLE OF CONTENTS

INTRODUCTION

The stories in this book are true. In some cases, the truth has been edited. The names of students and many other people have been changed. This book is not the whole truth. My life, just like everybody else's, has some gloomy stories, but those don't fulfill the purpose of my book. This book shows that there is still goodness in the world. I hope readers will see that goodness with me, crack a smile, and maybe even laugh.

Schoolhouse

KAITLYN'S CAR

" I know I'm tardy again, but I think my car is on fire! I wouldn't be late if it weren't for that piece-of-junk car I have to drive." Kaitlyn entered first hour late again, making the big splash she usually made when she was tardy. The class and I were used to her tardiness, and we had her spiel about the car pretty much memorized. It was always the same theme—the junky car—with variations, today's variation being fire.

She handed me her pink tardy slip while we all told her not to be a drama queen and assured her that the car was not on fire. A few kind souls offered words of comfort and encouragement. Several cynical students, especially those who didn't have a car, advised her to quit complaining. The realists in the room told her to get up earlier. Kaitlyn got herself settled down, and we went back to having English class.

The class hadn't taken even half a page of notes before an office runner came to the room with a call card. He handed it to me, and I saw that it was for Kaitlyn. The office runner said, "She needs to come to the office right now. Her car's on fire!"

Kaitlyn's "piece-of-junk" car burned itself out in the high school parking lot that morning. Kaitlyn had seen it coming and did not mourn the death of the car. She was hardly ever tardy after that.

HITCHHIKING

My black 1973 Mercedes diesel sputtered and died, and with the momentum the car had left, I edged it to the side of the road. An attempt to restart failed. Mark and I had owned the once-glorious car for a few years; as the car had aged, it had become less charming and more problematic, just like some people, but nobody who would read this story. Eventually, my husband, who loved the car and couldn't give it up, used it as a farm vehicle, but it was years away from that role on this early November morning in 1991. At this point in its life, the Mercedes was the car I drove to work, and its temporarily ceasing to be a vehicle made my morning inconvenient.

The inconveniences that day were many. As my dad would say, I had more problems than a cat in a roomful of rocking chairs. Two inches of snow didn't go well with my teacher shoes, and the wind added a cutting edge to the cold. This unfortunate event with the car meant that I would be late to school. I was too far from town to walk, and cell phones were still in the future.

Another "big" factor was my size; I was due to give birth later in November. What's a girl to do? I had never hitchhiked before, and I didn't like the idea of getting in the car with the next random stranger who pulled up. What if it were a bad guy? Options, however, were nonexistent, so I said a prayer for safety and decided to wave down the next car that came along.

At 7:30 a.m. a country road is no thoroughfare, but eventually a car appeared in my rearview mirror. As I flagged the car down, I could tell it was a Buick. I felt better already. An elderly woman rolled down the passenger's window. "Do you need some help?"

"I do. My car broke down; if you could just take me to the church at the first intersection when we get to town, I can call someone or have somebody there take me to work. That's my church." I knew I'd be okay if I could get to my church.

The elderly couple who had stopped, strangers to me, invited me to get in the car. I got my bags, heaved my large self in, buckled up, breathed a warm sigh of relief, and looked to my left to find that I was sharing the back seat with an old friend. A familiar face looked good, even if it was on a cock-a-poo.

Buddy, the brown cock-a-poo sitting beside me, knew me through the animal clinic where I had worked since high school. As the kennel girl, I got to know the pets who boarded, but I rarely got to know their people. Buddy had been a frequent guest, and I clearly remembered the nametag on his cage: Buddy Baumgartner. Buddy and

I exchanged pleasantries, and then I focused on human contact.

"You must be the Baumgartners," I offered. Mrs. Baumgartner turned to eyeball the psychic they had just picked up, and Mr. Baumgartner slowed the car, questioning the wisdom of picking up hitchhikers.

"How do you know us?" Mrs. Baumgartner asked, a little suspiciously.

"Oh, I know Buddy. I work at the animal clinic." My day took a sharp turn toward better at that moment. Any friend of Buddy was a friend of the Baumgartners. We chatted as they took me to the church. I got a ride to work, called Mark, and he took care of the car. A small town can't be beat on a snowy morning when the car breaks down.

BACK IN A FLASH

Early in the class period, an office runner interrupted my teaching to hand me a call card. I glanced at it and saw that it was for Kyle Durman. Kyle is the third of four Durman boys; it was my pleasure to teach all of them. The pink color of the card indicated that he had a scheduled appointment and needed to leave the school. I teach high school, so the students have been around long enough to know the routine. I didn't say anything to Kyle as I walked back to his seat and handed him the card; I just kept teaching.

I was teaching a riveting lesson; undoubtedly, all of the students who were awake would agree. I was so into the lesson that I didn't think any more about Kyle and his call card until a few minutes later when I looked at the end of the back row and there he was, still sitting in his chair. I was so surprised to see him that I called him out in front of all the other students.

"Kyle, you were supposed to go up to the office and check out! You have an appointment!" I know Kyle's mother, and as a mom myself, I stood in for her to make sure her boy didn't miss his appointment.

"I already went," he said.

"What?"

"I already went and now I'm back." He smiled at me through his tinseled teeth.

"Wait," I processed out loud, "you went up to the office and they said your appointment had been changed?"

"No, I went up to the office and checked out and went to my appointment and now I'm back. I put my sign-in slip on your desk."

"You're already back from your appointment? What kind of an appointment was it?" Now I was really behaving unprofessionally, asking Kyle personal questions in front of the whole class. My questions were driven by confusion, not contention, and Kyle took it all in stride (a quick stride, it turned out).

"I went to my orthodontist. It's right across the street. I walked over there, he tightened my braces, and I came back."

I scurried over to my desk and looked at his slip. Kyle had punched the sign-out clock to leave, gone to his orthodontist, and signed back in at school all in thirteen minutes. No wonder I was confused. That boy didn't want to miss another minute of English. I congratulated him on setting a land speed record for going to an appointment, and now that the fog had cleared, we went back to *Antigone*.

I kept the slip he left on my desk. It's been stapled on my bulletin board for years. If a student tries to take advantage of me by staying out of class too long "in the bathroom," I tell him he could have been to the orthodontist and back in that amount of time. Sometimes students scoff; I just show them Kyle's sign-in slip. It's nice to have proof.

GETSUB GRIEF

G etting a substitute teacher on a sick day is a process that has evolved during my thirty years of teaching. When I started teaching, we were required to call the school secretary on the morning of our illness. Good school secretaries can be intimidating; I always tried extra hard to sound weak and wheezy.

One year, and only one, we had to call the principal; he tired of that responsibility. In the fall of 2014, our school corporation switched to a new program called GetSub.

GetSub is in charge of getting substitute teachers. In this way, school corporations can outsource substitute teacher payrolls. This outsourcing magic began to happen about the same time the President pulled out his wand called Obamacare.

GetSub is all online. The substitutes register online, and then teachers go online and notify GetSub if they are going to be absent. GetSub isn't wonderful, and often a teacher wonders if a sub will show up. Often, no substitute will take the job when a teacher wakes up ill and posts the job on the morning of the illness. We have learned to post an illness in GetSub the night before, never mind the chance of getting better overnight.

Another problem is that sometimes substitutes sign up for the job but do not actually appear at the school. (The value of good substitute teachers is not to be underestimated, especially those brave and caring souls who show up consistently enough to get to know the kids by name.) In the event that a sub doesn't show up, other regular teachers are asked to give up their preparation hour to cover the absent teacher's classes.

Sometimes, only GetSub knows a teacher is absent. This is problematic. When the bell rings to begin class, the students look around the room to discover that no adult is present with them. In most scenarios this would represent loss of learning, safety concerns, or legal nightmares. Thank goodness, students at our high school have usually been mature enough to call the office or go tell the teacher next door when they realize they are unsupervised.

One day as my study hall was beginning, a student named William walked into the room, stopped at my desk, and said, "Mrs. Goggin, my class didn't have a teacher last hour."

"Really? How long was it before the sub showed up?" I asked nonchalantly as I took attendance.

"No, we didn't have a teacher all hour!"

"Whose class are you in?"

"Mrs. Carmony's class. We knew she was going to be gone today, but she said she would have a sub."

Now I was all ears. Mrs. Carmony had been my own English teacher in high school; she was also my department chair, my mentor, and my friend. I knew she had planned this absence well in advance. "What did you do? Did anybody call the office?"

"No, nobody called the office."

Troubled, I pried for details. "What happened? What did the class do? Did anything crazy happen that we should know about?"

Sometimes the truth is stranger than fiction. William couldn't have come up with a better answer if he had tried. He said, "We just did our work. We had a paper to write, and it was due at the end of the hour. We didn't have time to goof around."

After some investigation, I found out that the substitute who had signed up for the day had never shown up. Other teachers were asked to cover Mrs. Carmony's classes, and that worked out, except for fifth hour. Somehow the fifth hour class "fell through the cracks," all twenty-seven of them.

I shared this terrible and wonderful scoop with Mrs. Carmony as we walked down the hall together before school the next morning. First we blamed Obama for Get-Sub. After we got that out of the way, we both admitted it was remarkable that the students just did their work. Shirley wasn't as shocked as I was. She said, "They're seniors, so they're more mature, and they're good kids." She gave each of the fifth-hour students a fun-sized candy bar as a reward for not having fun—and doing their work—during their unsupervised hour.

I've been in teaching long enough to admit that some teachers can't control the students even when they are in the room with kids. Shirley Carmony, on the other hand, had control of the class even when she was absent. She's retired now, and she will never be replaced.

WE'LL FIND THEM SOMEWHERE

Since I have been teaching for thirty years, I'm getting the hang of it. I have the lessons laid out; the class website, a Moodle page, meticulously managed; and the kids under control. Despite my wisdom and experience, a new problem has developed as I face the classroom in my fifties. My professors at the Ball State Teachers College didn't cover this, perhaps because they were too young to understand, but it's a problem that can bring a lesson to a screeching halt. Teachers older than fifty need to know how to keep track of their reading glasses.

Those of us who need them and can't find them are doomed from the minute the bell rings to start the class. Taking attendance isn't going to happen without them, at least for those of us who still use the tiny boxes in the spiral-bound gradebook. Further, it's not possible to read the literature book or worksheet if the glasses are gone. I have learned to keep one pair on the desk, one pair on the rolling cart I teach from, and one pair on my head. It's good to have backup specs. I typically take them off or push them up when I'm not reading, only looking at students over my "readers" when I really need to give them the aging English teacher stink eye.

One late September day during fifth hour, I taught a class of sophomores, mesmerizing them, of course, until the bell was about to ring. I roamed the room as I taught, pausing beside random students to teach a little while before moving to the next spot. I must have hovered extensively beside Mandy at the front corner desk. She's a sweet girl who can be counted on to look up and smile at me instead of giving off teacher-repellant vibes.

As the bell rang to end the class, Mandy came to my desk with a very concerned look in her un-bespectacled eyes. "Mrs. Goggin, I've lost my glasses! I don't know how I could have lost them. I've just been sitting here the whole time. I can't read without my glasses. I have to have them for my next class!"

I'm an old teacher; it takes a lot to rattle me, so words of assurance came easily. "Let's just look around a little bit, Mandy. I'm sure we'll find them somewhere."

We moved books and papers and checked in every logical place. True to my prediction, it wasn't long before I began to see the situation clearly. I said, "Mandy, I think I might be wearing them. Could these be yours?"

I took the glasses off the top of my head, held them out, and received Mandy's confused smile in exchange. She put them on as I rushed her off to her next class.

I later told her I would try not to do it again, but when a teacher is old enough to need reading glasses, absent-mindedness usually shows up too. Besides, it worked out pretty well: They were the right prescription, and they were stylish. Too bad we found them.

PRAYER IN SCHOOL

The last hour of the last day of the last week before Christmas break had arrived. The first semester was ending, but we were not feeling festive yet. My seventh hour class was facing a comprehensive final exam.

Since the class—a group of sixteen honors seniors—was so small, I had been able to run the class with more ease than I would have with a larger class, and I got to know the kids. Further, Sam, Brent, Molly, and Audrey's siblings had graced my class rosters in the past, so I felt as if I already knew them. I had graded reflective essays and personal narratives their siblings had written about their families. English teachers know a lot about family lives. This makes Back-to-School Night far more interesting to the English teacher than it is to other teachers; we can put behaviors with names and faces. Just saying.

Anyway, in addition to knowing the siblings, I knew the parents of many of these students. Twenty or so years previously, Tristen, Edmond, and Sam's fathers had suffered their same torture. Tyler, Shayla, and Hope's fathers *and* mothers had been my high school students. Some of the kids looked and acted so much like their parents I inadvertently called them by their parents' names most of the semester. For the record, I have already decided that if a student ever says, "You taught my grandma," I am going straight to the office to retire.

This group of kids was a pleasure to teach. Although some of them weren't at the top academically, they were tops in terms of respect and cooperation. As we ended this dreaded semester of research and grammar, every student had turned in both the rough draft and final copy of the big research paper with minimal prodding from me. They had all stood in front of the class and given a three-to-six-minute presentation. They had stuck with me through the passive verbs, retained objects, infinitives, and noun clauses. It had been a sweet semester, and the final exam would end it, for better or worse.

As the class gathered and got settled before the exam, I overheard their murmurings. Some admitted to their pals that they should have studied more. Brent, a baseball player, told Molly that he had studied a lot; Molly had too.

The students got into Moodle on their computers, scrolled down to the final exam, and became silent in readiness for me to give the password. I stood at the back of the class so that I could see when their screens were ready. As I opened my mouth to give the password, Brent turned around in his seat, looked at me, and said in a voice loud enough for the whole class to hear, "Mrs. Goggin, I'm really nervous about this test. Can we pray before we take it?" Several others in the class agreed.

I wish I could have led them in a prayer. Instead, I said, "You can pray. There's nothing stopping you. You could have been praying all day long. This is finals week, so I'm sure many prayers have gone up from this building. God has probably heard a lot of unfamiliar voices today."

A few of the kids chuckled at my last line. Some seemed to like the idea of whispering a prayer on their own.

Brent said, "Oh yeah, I guess I could."

I gave the password, and they trudged through the test. I don't know how many of the students in the room whispered a prayer, but I do know how the scores came out. Brent had the highest score in the class!

His studying surely contributed to his success, but I think Brent and I would agree that he had some help. I couldn't send a boy to the office for cheating by getting help from God on his final exam, nor did I want to. When I saw Brent again after Christmas break, I congratulated him on his score and told him that his hard work and prayer had turned out to be a winning combination.

SPIRITS

The room to my right just past the bathrooms is a special education classroom. My neighbor, Mrs. Smith, has my respect for many reasons. She doesn't get rattled, enjoys her work, and likes the students she teaches. She has an aura of strength about her. I would want her on my side in an altercation. Further, she seems to know how to handle the varying situations that play out in her room.

As a case in point, here's what happened one morning toward the end of first semester. We all needed a break, some more than others. A student named Phillip was in our hallway before the school day started. He was holding an invisible tool of some kind; judging by the way he was wielding it, the device was something like a television remote. He was directing it to various walls and corners. My neighbor to the left, Sean Slagle, stopped Phillip in the hall to ask him what he was doing.

"I'm detecting spirits," Phillip answered, trying to stay focused on his job.

"Found anything?" Mr. Slagle asked.

"Not yet."

During passing period at the end of first hour, Jim Nicholson, our school security officer, saw Sean in the hall. He said, "I've been a policeman for twenty years, but I did something for the first time today. Mrs. Smith called and said she needed me and the principal. We came down to assist her, and I handcuffed and arrested a spirit and removed it from the premises. It seemed like the best way to handle the situation."

Kudos to special education teachers, and thanks to school security officers who keep their hands on the pulse of the school and take out the bad guys, both real and imagined.

KIDS THESE DAYS

Forty-four names on my study hall roster meant I would have to leave my classroom to supervise the group. Destination: east cafeteria, which was a favorable destination for two reasons. One was that it had good reception for all the electronic devices that keep students happy. The second reason was the room was large enough that I could keep the students apart from each other, which kept talking to a minimum. I favor a silent study hall.

On the flip side, the cafeteria study hall had some unfavorable aspects. One drawback was that I had to carry my computer and papers and miscellaneous junk up to the cafeteria every day and get set up before I could even take attendance. Pulling everything but the kitchen sink out of my bag, I felt like Mary Poppins. Whew!

The worst problem—it was a biggie—was the condition of the tables when my study hall arrived for sixth hour. First, second, and third lunch groups had just dined on those tables. When the bell rang to release third lunch, my study hall poured into the cafeteria. The tables were a sticky mess. Most of the tables featured remnants of the dreaded school cafeteria lunch—French fries, ketchup, mustard, cardboard pizza crusts, grease smears, or used napkins. I'm pretty sure a herd of swine sat at the table I used.

The first day the study hall met, I didn't want to put my books down because the table I had chosen as my station was so icky. I put my books on a chair. After introducing myself to the group, I apologized for the condition of the tables. I explained that Steve, the school custodian, was sorry too, but he couldn't possibly clean all of the tables in five minutes. Next, I talked about my study hall rules and procedures. My spiel ended with "If anyone would be willing to clean the tables every day, come talk to me. That would be great."

That night sleep escaped me as I thought about the messy tables. In retrospect, I realized that asking if one student would want to clean all of the tables every day was one of the top five dumbest things I have ever said. What kid would do that? I sure wasn't going to. I had work to do.

That's when God turned on the light of common sense in my brain. The simple answer was to ask the students if they would be willing to do it one day, turning our large attendance into an advantage.

The next morning, I saw Steve and told him I thought we had the problem solved. When he heard my idea, he chuckled and wished me a doubtful "Good luck."

Sixth hour rolled around, and I greeted my students at their dirty tables. I shared my idea of students volunteering to clean the tables one day, taking turns. Then I took my class list and went around the room to ask people individually if I could count on them to help. Don't guess too low. Of the forty-four I asked, forty said yes. When I told Steve, his eyes lit up and he said, "You're kidding!"

The next day as I gathered my bag and headed to the cafeteria, I wondered whom I would ask to go first, realizing it might be awkward for the first person. I decided I would volunteer first. That didn't happen, though, because when I got there, I found a sweet girl named Alli already on the job. I was tempted to tell her not to clean the tables of the four people who refused to help, but then I remembered we all need grace, so their tables were washed every day along with the others.

When she was finished, I asked her if any of the kids had said thank you. They had. From that day on, I just went down the class roster with the gloves, the bucket, and the cleaning rags.

Thus began our semester of volunteerism. On Friday of the first week of school, I had to be gone, so I asked a varsity basketball player, Tristen, if he would clean the tables that day even though I wouldn't be there.

He said, "Sure, no problem," and followed through.

Some days the student I asked might say, "I have a lot of homework today. Can I do it tomorrow?" That always worked out.

A student named Alex was added to the study hall. After I explained the rules and procedures, I told him that in this study hall we take turns cleaning the tables.

He replied, "That doesn't really make sense to me, Mrs. Goggin, but I'll do it for you."

Some students, like Sidney (who had lots of energy and little homework) volunteered for extra turns. I took my turn at the end of the roster. Some of the students (shy little Madison, for one) said, "Mrs. Goggin, you don't have to do that. I'll do it for you." I thanked her but told her I needed to take my turn.

By the end of the semester, most of us had cleaned the tables twice, and some had done it three times. Much of what the public hears about teenagers is worrisome. As a high school teacher, I have the inside scoop on how teenagers are acting, and I have plenty of good stories to tell about kids these days.

RESTROOM GRAFFITI

Once in a while, our school has an outbreak of restroom graffiti. These outbreaks are usually short lived. Thank goodness our students get limited satisfaction from sneaking up on a stall door with a marker.

When graffiti appears in a restroom, the assistant principals sometimes take a picture of it and send it to the staff as an email to see if any of the teachers recognize the handwriting. Remarkably, this works.

One email we got contained a picture of the following memorable dialogue from a girls' restroom wall. The first line was a large threatening scrawl; the second line, obviously by a different person, was small, neat, and even punctuated.

I'M GOING TO KILL SOMEBODY

Start with the math teachers, please.

I don't remember if the assistant principals solved that one or not, but the auxiliary benefit of sending the picture in an email was the years of snickering it provided for the staff—most of us, anyway.

PRAYER REQUESTS

I've had it easy. Our school has had a history of good discipline since the early eighties. Effective policies and high expectations have stopped many problems before they started, thank God. Most of my career has been a student holding the door for me when I walk into the building in the morning, a student saying "Hi, Mrs. Goggin!" as I stand in the hall during passing periods, and a student saying "How's your day going?" as I take attendance and start the class.

Most misbehaving students respond well if I walk over to them and quietly say, "I need for you to take it down a notch," or just catch their eye and give them the "zip your lips" signal from across the room. Some students need consequences, but it usually doesn't take much.

Unfortunately, a few notable exceptions come to mind. The worst class I ever had was a fourth period group of sophomores I tried to teach several years ago. I didn't get to teach that group much; most of the semester was spent on crowd control. It was a bad mix of students, and by the end of the semester, a full 40 percent of the class had been expelled (not just suspended) from school. I seldom dread a class, but I dreaded that one. I felt as if I were in Dante's *Inferno* fifty minutes a day, and I only got through it by prayers and pure grit.

The most famous confrontation I had with a student (he was not in the aforementioned awful class) involved a smart remark, a write-up, a prayer, and New Mexico. Rocco had been problematic for most of the semester, but he was in rare form one fall Friday as I was trying to teach.

I stopped the lesson several times and asked him to quit talking. Given a few more years of experience, I could have handled him better, but I was young, and he continued to be disruptive. After fruitless efforts to settle him down, I wrote him up and told him to go to the office.

To my surprise, Rocco announced—for the benefit of the whole class—that he would be happy to go to the office because he really wanted to get away from his awful English teacher. I knew he was going to get more than he wanted in the assistant principal's office; nevertheless, his behavior and his parting remark had their intended shock effect on me. I was troubled by the whole incident the rest of the day and throughout the weekend.

On Sunday at church during open prayer time, I went forward to have someone agree with me in prayer for Rocco. We specifically prayed that I wouldn't have a bad attitude toward him and that he wouldn't ruin the class anymore and that the whole ugly situation would be resolved peacefully.

On Monday, Rocco was absent, and the class proceeded smoothly. On Tuesday his seat was still empty. Wednesday, Thursday, and Friday passed with no Rocco sightings. After two whole weeks of his absence, I thought he must be awfully sick. I went to the office to ask about him and see if I should prepare a makeup work packet for someone in his family to pick up. When I asked about him, the secretary laughed and said, "No, you don't need to send work home. Rocco McDaniels moved to New Mexico."

"Moved to New Mexico? Really? When did that happen?" I asked.

"Oh, I guess we forgot to tell you. He moved almost two weeks ago. They just picked up and moved."

When I told that story at lunch, people laughed so hard they nearly choked on their Lean Cuisines. Their laughter was followed by some reverential thoughts about the power of prayer.

Soon after that, teachers began to tell me the names of students they wanted me to pray for. My department chair requested prayer for a teacher or two, and one former department member accused me of praying him into early retirement. I assured him I had not targeted him in any disappearance prayers. Off the record, a staff member approached me about praying for a particular principal.

I'm not taking responsibility for anybody's disappearance, but I will say that when I found out Rocco McDaniels had moved to New Mexico the day after I had prayed for a peaceful resolution, it was a pretty sweet answer to prayer.

WHAT'S IN A NAME?

A tall, lanky blonde came into my classroom, found his name, Jeremy Matthews, on the seating chart, and figured out where to sit. This was the third hour of the first day of school. Throughout my rules-and-procedures talk, Jeremy was polite and attentive. Later in the day, I saw him again. His name appeared on my sixth-hour study hall list, and he showed up and took a seat, a slightly familiar face in the sea of faces I had never seen before.

The next day as I took attendance during third hour, I looked at the seating chart and then looked at the students while I said their names, trying to connect names with faces. I looked at Jeremy's name on the seating chart and said, "Hmm, aren't you in my study hall?"

"Yes," he replied.

"For some reason I wanted to call you Jameson, but I can see on the seating chart that you are Jeremy."

"Yeah, I get that a lot."

On the third day of school, I took attendance without the seating chart, trying to test my memory. I got to the Matthews boy and said, "I'm going to get it right this time. I ought to know who you are. I see you all the time. You're Jeremy."

He smiled. "No, I'm Jameson." He was a patient and friendly kid, thank goodness. At this point, I was thinking retirement might not be far off. Thirty years of names might be too many. How could I not remember this kid's name? He was in my class and my study hall. I seemed to see him in the hall twice as much as I saw other kids. I was embarrassed. My vision for the first week of school didn't include me coming off as an overwrought senile dingbat.

"I am so sorry I can't get your name right. I don't know why I'm having so much trouble."

"That's okay; you're not the only one," he reassured his new old English teacher.

In the whirlwind of starting a new year, much to my chagrin, I got the name wrong all week. Meanwhile, my classes had read W. D. Wetherell's "The Bass, the River, and Sheila Mant," and quizzed over it. I entered Jeremy's grade in the third-hour roster, and when I got to the fifth-hour roster, a floodlight came on in the cavernous recesses of my dimly-lit brain. I found myself entering a grade for Jameson Matthews. No wonder I was confused; there were two of him.

On Monday, I correctly called Jeremy by name both in third hour and during sixth hour study hall. I identified Jameson correctly during fifth hour. I mentioned to each of them separately that it might have helped if I had known they were identical twins. They gave identical answers: "I thought you already knew." Well, it does seem obvious in hindsight.

Jeremy and Jameson were "a pleasure to have in class," as we used to say on report cards. After I got to know them, in a tiny moment of unprofessionalism I suggested to them that if one was good at math and the other better at English, they could just swap classes. They laughed and didn't seem to take my brilliant idea very seriously. At least I don't think they did. How would I know?

BACK-TO-SCHOOL NIGHT

As a high school teacher, I have a love-hate relationship with Back-to-School Night. I love seeing my former students as parents. I hate the idea that the parents feel obligated to come to school for this event when their children are knocking on the door of adulthood and can fend for themselves.

The latest trend is for Back-to-School Night to happen during the first or second week of school. On one hand, getting it out of the way early is nice, but on the other hand, the teachers don't even know the kids yet, so when a parent says, "I'm Tasha's dad," a layer of meaninglessness is exposed. All I can say about Tasha at that point is "I must be Tasha's teacher."

This evening of hospitality makes for a long day. I get to school around 7:30 a.m. Then I teach all day. The beginning of the year is always exhausting. I have to front-load a lot of information to the students, and we're still working out classroom management and how to get along. By the end of the school day, I'm tired. Because of living so far away, I don't have time to go home and come back, so I just stay and work in my room.

By six o'clock, Back-to-School Night has started, an evening of meet and greet. I have been teaching since Abraham Lincoln was a boy, so a lot of the parents who come to this event are my former students. In many cases, I remember where they sat in class, what they wrote their research papers about, what sport they played, and their personalities. In other cases, greeting a former student as a parent is problematic. I remember these people as sixteen-year-olds, and time, gravity, and calories have produced a person who bears little or no resemblance to the adolescent I knew. The situation is confusing and awkward, but we get through it.

One year our principal urged the entire staff to attend a volleyball match to top off Back-to-School Night. Volleyball started at 7:30 p.m. in the fieldhouse. Despite my age and experience, I continue to take these directives seriously, so I went to the volleyball match. The teachers who attended were allowed to put their names in a bowl for door prizes. Names were to be randomly drawn, but only teachers could enter.

Somewhere toward the end of the second set, I saw something very interesting going on in the "volleyball mom" section of seats. Three of the moms had the bowl and were taking the names out, reading them, and folding them back up. Exhausted and grumpy, I tapped the equally frazzled teacher next to me and said, "Look at that. See what they are doing? That's not fair!" She agreed; it was shady business: hand-picking a random winner. All three of the moms were my former students. I thought about walking down to tell them to stop doing that, but I controlled myself.

The set ended a few minutes later, and it was time for the door prizes. The way the drawing had been handled didn't seem so bad when I heard the announcer say, "Annette Goggin, come down and get your door prize." A whole bunch of nice loot was a great way to end a long day.

PREGNANT

First semester was more than half gone. The air was crisp, the leaves were beautiful, and the students were back from fall break, all in their places with bright happy faces. Well, most of them were in their places, and a few of them were smiling as they started the countdown to Christmas break. A couple of English teachers came back from fall break with news that could have easily wiped the bright happy face off our principal.

Early in the day, one of our younger English teachers went to the principal's office during her prep hour to tell him that she would need to be on maternity leave from spring break until the end of the school year. He's a positive guy and was genuinely happy for her.

From a strictly educational perspective, the maternity leave was problematic. Ninth-grade teachers play a very important role in getting students ready to pass the End-of-Course Assessment at the tenth-grade level. Now a ninth-grade teacher would have to be replaced by a substitute for nine weeks.

Sixth hour of the same day, a first-year teacher also went to Mr. Wilkin's office, excited but reluctant to share the news that she would need to take a maternity leave from spring break until the end of her first year of teaching. Now a tenth-grade teacher would have to be replaced during the last nine weeks of school.

A less optimistic principal might have been despondent. Not one, but two critical English teachers would be doing Lamaze breathing in the hospital instead of getting the students ready for the ECA at the school. Mr. Wilkin maintained his smile and kept calm. He assured her he would be able to find a good sub.

Two of nine English teachers broke their joyous news in one day. In my thirty years at the school, we have never had more than one English teacher pregnant at a time. The situation was unprecedented, and it led me to give birth to a pretty good prank.

I emailed the rest of the department and set the plan in place. The next day, the rest of the English department and a few other random teachers emailed Mr. Wilkin during their prep. All of them were pregnant and would be needing a maternity leave. A fifty-something teacher wrote that she and her husband were both shocked and thrilled. A single teacher was worried, embarrassed, and greatly concerned that her mother would kill her. Another young teacher was concerned that she and her husband would not be able to make ends meet with another mouth to feed. The best email was sent by Mr. Prater.

Mr. Wilkin,

Just wanted to give you a heads up that I had a doctor's appointment Friday. I have not been feeling well lately, so they ran some tests Friday, and the results came back today. This may sound strange, but the doctor insists that I am pregnant! It is a very rare condition that happens when the wife wears the pants in the relationship. Just wanted to let you know.

Thanks, Luther

Mr. Wilkin was onto our prank immediately and saw fit to reply to all of us with plenty of smart remarks.

Just before spring break, the English department gave the truly pregnant teachers a baby shower in the teachers' lounge one day after school. Of course, we all attended in various stages of pregnancy, depending on what we could find in our classrooms to put under our shirts. Mr. Wilkin wasn't at the shower, but we sent him a picture of the prolific English department.

In case anyone is wondering, two healthy babies were born shortly after spring break. We were able to find good substitute teachers, and when the ECA scores came back, they were just fine.

Church House

TAPESTRY

My grandfather, Jacob Kersten, left the Netherlands and arrived in America in 1913. Christina Hendricks, my grandmother, also left the Netherlands and immigrated through Ellis Island by herself in 1919. She was twenty-three years old. They each found their way to Nebraska, where Christina located her friend from Holland, Dena Kersten. Dena was Jacob's sister, and she introduced the two in Nebraska.

A few months later, while Christina was visiting relatives in Idaho, Jake wrote her a letter asking her to marry him. He got a "yes" letter in reply, and they tied the knot in 1920.

A few months later, they homesteaded and started a family in Mellette County, South Dakota. My two uncles, Leonard and Myron, were born there. Later, they moved to a farm near Wheaton, Kansas, where my mother, Edith, was born. Eventually, they all ended up in Percival, Iowa.

When my mother was a youngster in Iowa, her dad worked for a farmer, and her family lived in the farmhand's house. The owner needed some work done on the house, and Mr. Mullinax was the carpenter who showed up. He saw that there was a little girl in the house, so he brought his daughters with him the next time he came. That's how my mother became friends with the two Mullinax girls.

Every Sunday, the Mullinax family travelled all the way from Percival to Tabor, Iowa, to attend the Nazarene church. The girls would bring my mother Sunday school papers, and one week she read a poem about being saved. Edith, who was seven at the time, asked her mother, "What does it mean to be saved?"

Her mother was doing dishes at the kitchen sink. Tears began to roll down her cheeks as she answered in her heavy accent, "Ach, I don't know. It's vat da Mullinax people believe in."

"Is it what we're supposed to believe?" Edith asked.

"I don't know," was all Christina could say. My mother had heard radio preachers, but the Mullinaxes were the first real people she ever heard talk about having a saving relationship with Jesus Christ. Not long after that, the Mullinax family moved away. She found out later that they had continued to pray for her for years.

Even before Christina knew Christ as her Savior, my grandma had respect for God. In the early 1940s—before they started going to church regularly—my grandma and my mother would sit by the radio and listen to Charles E. Fuller's "Old-Fashioned Revival Hour" and respectfully kneel during the radio prayers. When Christina would try to get Myron, a teenaged boy, to listen to the broadcast, he sometimes joined them, but grumbled, "You're not going to make a preacher out of me." I think that's when God chuckled and said, "We'll see."

Later, when my mother, Edith, was in high school, some of their country neighbors, Pauline and Larry Snyder, invited the Kerstens to go to church with them across the river in Nebraska City, Nebraska. By this time, Myron and Leonard had joined the Army, and Edith was the only child still at home.

My grandparents had a car, but money was tight. Gas was rationed because of the war, and the bridge across the Missouri River into Nebraska was a toll bridge. The Snyders picked them up for church every Sunday. At the Free Methodist Church in Nebraska City, my grandma finally understood what it meant to be saved. That is where my grandparents and my mother went to the altar at the front of the sanctuary, confessed their sins, received the salvation Christ offers, and had the assurance that their sins were forgiven.

Meanwhile, Myron was stationed in the Philippines with the Army Corps of Engineers during World War II. There, he attended a GI Gospel Hour and heard a Rev. Pitts preach a sermon about a choice between heaven and hell. Rev. Pitts knew that many of the men in the audience would be facing gunfire soon. Myron liked what he heard.

Talking to the preacher after the service, he found out Rev. Pitts was a Nazarene. When the war ended, Myron found his way to a Nazarene church in Louisiana, dedicated his life to Christ, and heard God's call to preach. His next move was to Bethany Nazarene College in Bethany, Oklahoma. By the time he retired, Myron had been a Nazarene pastor for fifty years.

My mother ended up at Bethany Nazarene College by way of her brother Myron. At Bethany, she met a skinny guy from western Oklahoma. He had hitchhiked to college with a suitcase, a twenty-dollar bill, a will to work, and a call to preach. A couple of years later, they were married, and my mom, who had been given Nazarene Sunday school papers as a small child, became a Nazarene pastor's wife.

Two Dutch immigrants and their children, a carpenter and his daughters, some country neighbors who shared their car, a GI Gospel Hour preacher, and a skinny kid from southwest Oklahoma are all carefully woven into a tapestry of God's grace. What else would we expect?

USE WHAT YOU HAVE

My dad was born in Harlingen, Texas—just this side of the Rio Grande—in 1930. When he was still an infant, the family moved to Tillman County, Oklahoma, which put them just on the Oklahoma side of the Red River.

The Dust Bowl was more than a history lesson for them. Partly as a result of the weather, the family was very poor. My grandfather, William Daniel Asbury Johnson, was a sharecropper; he also took odd jobs wherever he could find them. My grandmother, Lillie Johnson, helped on the farm and took care of the children: Nelson, Spencer, Louise, and Garland (my daddy). They barely scratched a living out of the red dust they called home. One year, my dad's Christmas gifts were an orange and a pencil, and he was glad to get them.

The kids went to school, but they worked, too. When my dad was just ten years old and his sister, Louise, was fifteen, they picked cotton for a neighbor. They dragged the heavy sacks down the rows, filling them again and again until they had earned enough money to buy a second-hand couch for their mother. That is the same couch where my dad would see his mother kneeling in the living room a few years later on the nights when he had been out past his curfew and tried to sneak in. I am happy that it is in my living room now.

When my Uncle Spencer was fifteen, he asked his mother if he could be in 4-H. A lot of the kids at school were in 4-H, and it sounded like fun. She wanted him to be in the club, but it seemed that they were too poor for him to compete. A 4-Her has to have something to show, but their family had nothing good enough. None of their livestock was show quality. Most of the other projects involved making something, and there was no money to buy materials or a show-quality animal.

The obvious answer seemed to be "No, we have nothing to work with," but my grandma thought and prayed about it first. She came up with an idea. She said, "Spencer, you have nothing to work with and nothing to show at the fair, but God gave everyone a voice. You can use what you have." Thus, Spencer joined the 4-H club, signed up for the speech competition, and won at the local level with a speech called "Home." Next was the state competition in Oklahoma City.

His speech was perfected, but he faced a new problem as he prepared to go to the big city: His shoes had holes in them and weren't fit to wear to the state competition.

Again, his mother found a way. Louise, who was twelve at the time, had the nicest shoes in the family and they were big enough to fit Spencer, but they were saddle oxfords. If

Spencer wore them for the competition, everyone would know he was wearing his sister's shoes. That little problem was solved with some black shoe polish.

Now Spencer had shoes to wear, but what about Louise? She had joined the speech competition, too, and won the girls' division, so she also got to go to the state competition. Their mother gave her shoes to Louise. They were too small and pinched Louise's feet so that she got blisters, but it was all for a good cause.

As it turns out, Spencer—with his polished shoes and polished speech—was pretty good at using what God gave him. He won at the state level and got to ride on a train to go to nationals in Chicago with his 4-H leader.

Shortly after the speech contest, Spencer realized why he had been given his speaking gift when he felt God's call to preach. As a fifteen-year-old, he began preaching wherever he could find an audience. Now that my Uncle Spencer is ninety-four, it's easy to take a backward glance at his life and see that the 4-H speech competition was a harbinger of a lifetime of travelling the world to preach.

Uncle Spencer and his family never lived close to ours when I was growing up, but I did get to hear him preach once when I was a kid and remember the text (God is looking for a man to stand in the gap) and the passion of his preaching. I can see why he won the contest. That boy wearing his sister's shoes ended up preaching in fifteen countries. Even into their nineties, Uncle Spencer and Aunt Delene would drive all over the United States in their Oldsmobile so that he could preach at camp meetings and revivals. Yielding only to their physical limitations, Uncle Spencer and Aunt Delene have finally slowed down.

My Aunt Louise, now ninety-one, whose shoes helped get the whole thing started, proudly recalled the story about Spencer's success at the 4-H contest, ending with a chuckle and a sisterly remark: "Spencer got the trip and I got the blisters."

WAITING ROOMS AND SANCTUARIES

M y dad is not around to defend himself since he has
moved (specifically, to heaven), but considering his
current location, I don't think he gives a hoot if we have a
good laugh at his expense. That said, I'm going to tell on
my dad.

His second pastorate was a tiny church in Hope, Arkansas. My parents lived in one side of a duplex; the other
side was the church sanctuary, Sunday school rooms, fel-
lowship hall, and church office, all in three rooms.

One way my dad and mom added to the church attendance was by having children. My brother was born at
Hope, so church attendance showed a significant percent-
age jump that year. My sister was born during my dad's
pastorate at Capitol Hill in Oklahoma City, and I "discovered America" (as my dad would say) another four years
later, making me a Sooner too.

Garland Johnson was the kind of pastor who called on the church people (he went to their homes to offer encouragement and prayer) and visited the sick in the hospitals. Sometimes he would take one of us kids along to give my mother a break. At this point in our family life, Margaret was an infant, and I hadn't come along yet, so Mark was the only candidate to tag along. Mark was obedient and mature for five, and the world seems to have been a safer place in 1960. Ironically, the combination of those characteristics contributed to an unfortunate event.

One of the flock was a patient at Mercy Hospital, and my dad wanted to pay a visit. He took Mark along. Daddy knew the visit would be short, and a hospital room is no place for a five-year-old, so he explained to Mark that he could sit in the waiting room in the front lobby. Mark had brought some toys and coloring books, so he was pleased with the plan. This was a routine they had done before, and Mark knew that he could go to the nun who watched over the lobby if he needed anything.

Daddy made his visit, said a prayer, and left. He didn't just leave the room; he left the hospital. As he strode through the waiting room and out the door, his mind must have been full of the many things he needed to remember.

His drive across the city was pleasant enough, but when Daddy walked in the door at home, his welcome was short lived. It didn't take my mother long to notice someone was missing.

"Where's Mark?" she gasped. My dad isn't here today to explain this story, but I'm thinking his trip back to the hospital wasn't nearly as pleasant as his drive home had been. He found Mark in the waiting room in the care of a nun. Mark had played with his toys and colored for a really long time, but had finally begun to whimper a few minutes before my dad got back to the hospital. Mark hadn't gone into a full-blown cry, but he sure was glad to see his daddy.

Miscommunication gets the blame for the second verse of this same song. Mark was eight years old this time; Margaret was three; I was a newborn. The Sunday night service had ended, and Mother was eager to get Margaret and me to bed. The parsonage was only a couple of blocks from the Capitol Hill church, so my mom asked one of the church folk if they would give the three of us a ride. She told my dad she was going on home, and off we went. Daddy saw Mother leave the building with me and Margaret. Mark usually played tag with the other boys in the summer twilight after the evening service, so my dad assumed my mom had rounded him up as she left. She, on the other hand, assumed he would bring Mark home.

An important detail in this snafu was that Mark wasn't playing in the church yard. He had fallen asleep during the service and had eventually toppled over so that he was half sitting, half lying on his side in the pew. My dad visited with people until the last lingerers were gone, scanned the sanctuary before he turned out the lights, and locked the church doors in the growing darkness. Then he went home. As soon as he walked in the door, he was greeted with a succinct question he had heard before. "Where's Mark?" When my dad got back to the church, Mark was still in dreamland, so he suffered no ill effect from his brief abandonment.

My mom and dad told him what had happened, and Mark learned a lesson that has stuck with him for fifty-some years. I'd bet my next tithe check he never falls asleep in church.

FAITH, CHILD-SIZED

When I was an infant, my family moved from Oklahoma City to Columbus, Indiana. We left both sets of my grandparents in Oklahoma, so some years we would make a trip back during the Christmas season. This was well before minivans and SUVs hit the road. The station wagon was the biggest family vehicle available, and we didn't have one. Icy roads and frequent bathroom breaks meant slow going. It was a long trip for a family of five; we fussed a lot, so Mother would have us play the alphabet game or sing church songs to pass the time.

Since I was small and there weren't seat belt laws, it was easy for me to switch spots if I got bored. Sometimes I rode up front between my parents. Sometimes I sat in the back seat between my brother, Mark, and my sister, Margaret. Sometimes I curled up on the floor beneath my sister's seat so she could turn sideways and lean against the door while she read a book. Best of all, sometimes I would get to lie in the back window. It was an excellent spot at night when traffic was light and there were no headlights behind us to interfere with stargazing.

But I was most interested in having the back window vantage point during the day if my mother started singing the song "Surely Goodness and Mercy," which quotes Psalm 23. "Surely goodness and mercy shall follow me all the days of my life." That peppy song was one of my favorites. The idea of Shirley Goodness and her friend Mercy following us not only brought me comfort, but also magnetized me to the back window. I didn't expect the two of them to be in the car behind us, since no heavenly beings in the Bible ever showed up in a car, but I knew they must be running or flying somewhere behind us. A glimpse of Shirley and Mercy would have sent my faith right over the top.

I needed faith most at night. As a youngster, I was afraid of the dark. To help me go to sleep, my parents got me a Donald Duck nightlight; I liked looking at Donald in the darkness, but he didn't help me fall asleep. One of my parents, usually my mother, would lie beside me in the bed for a few minutes every night. My mother spoke often about how God is with us even when nobody else is. She assured me that I could go to sleep without worry, knowing that He is always taking care of me. She explained that even though I couldn't see God, I could feel His presence.

I was three years old when we took one of our Christmas trips to Oklahoma. We stopped at a mom-and-pop motel in Missouri. The room had two double beds and a rollaway: one bed for my parents, one for my sister and me, and the rollaway for my brother. I felt safe because I got to sleep with Margaret.

Mark, who was eleven at the time, wasn't thrilled about the rollaway. He started the night on the rollaway, but sometime during the night, he got so tired of the squeaks and lumps that he got in bed with me and my sister, pushing me to the middle.

The next morning at breakfast as Mark complained about the rollaway, Mother turned to me and said, "Did you know Mark got in bed with you and Margaret last night?"

Because of what I had been taught about God's presence, my three-year-old response made perfect sense to me. "I knew I felt somebody, but I thought it was God."

I'm too big to ride in the back window now, but looking back at the roads I've travelled, I can see that God's goodness and mercy have followed me, that's for sure.

JESUS LOVES ME

One of the first songs I learned as a child was "Jesus loves me, this I know, for the Bible tells me so. . . ." In case I didn't believe it just from the Bible stories I was told, Jesus loved me through the candy ladies at church who always had some Smarties or Clove gum for me, and through VBS craft helpers who helped me make a church house out of popsicle sticks, and through Sunday school teachers who made David and Goliath come to life on a Flannelgraph board.

Jesus loved me through Doug Slack, a song evangelist who always brought along a guitar and Jocko, his monkey puppet, who hid his head in Doug's arm, only coming out to look around and nod yes or no. In addition to bringing the guitar and Jocko, Doug Slack brought laughter with him. After the evening services during a revival, he would come to the parsonage, tell funny stories, and wiggle his ears. I got to sit at the grown-up table and stay up late, laughing myself silly.

Jesus loved me through Lester and Della Waggoner, my substitute grandparents, who let me come over to their house once a week when I was a preschooler. After we had lunch and I helped dry the dishes, we always went to Danner's dime store, where I got to pick out a little square Whitman story book. Then we would go back to their house on Elm Street, and Della would sit in her olive-green vinyl recliner with me on her lap and read the new book to me.

Jesus loved me through Velma Douglas, the church secretary, who always had time for the preacher's kid who lived next door, even though I tended to drop by for a little snack almost every day. Her specialty was a cracker with a squirt of cheese from a can, a novel treat at the time. Velma was even nice enough to extend hospitality to our family's cat, Happy, who also liked squirt cheese.

I want to know Christ, but I've never sat at the kitchen table and laughed at Him like I laughed at Doug Slack. I never got to go to Danner's dime store with Jesus like I did with Lester and Della. I've never eaten squirt cheese with Jesus in the church office like I did with Velma, but I think He would have been in the middle of it had He come to earth two thousand years later. I think Jesus must have been like these people because they so much wanted to be like Him.

CHURCH CAMP

My mom, dad, sister, and I sat on the back steps of the family dorm after the evening service. In the twilight of a mercilessly hot July day, Daddy sliced a cantaloupe, and then we swatted mosquitos while we ate, the juice running down our chins. Just happy. We were at the southwest Oklahoma district campground near Anadarko, and we were there for the whole week of camp meeting.

Camp meeting was a great time for me as a kid. It was a safe place, so I got to run around on my own. At certain times during the day and after every evening service, the snack shack was open. I had a little ticket, and the people who ran the snack shack punched holes in it as I got my snacks. We didn't go out to eat very often, and my parents didn't keep pop in our home except twice a year during revivals for the evangelists who came over after church, so I had limited exposure to soft drinks. The snack shack offered all manner of soft drinks. I soon established a favorite, red pop. My parents explained that the ticket would last all week if I got one soft drink each day. I thought I'd died and gone to heaven.

Red pop wasn't the only reason I was thinking of heaven. One morning a pouring rain pounded on the open-sided tabernacle during the morning service. The bad news was the roof leaked. The good news was it was raining in the middle of a hot, dry, Oklahoma summer. Moving out from under the drips, the congregation belted out "This is Like Heaven to Me" even louder. I don't know if it was a drought year or if we were just enjoying Jesus; either way, the rain and the song and the saints and the Spirit all made it seem like heaven.

The oppressive heat that returned after the rain and the ubiquitous snakes reminded us that we were not in heaven. In fact, they made us think of the other place. One night after an evening service, a girl was bitten by a rattlesnake. I was part of the crowd that huddled around her and saw the bite holes in her ankle before someone sped her to the emergency room in Anadarko. She lived to tell about it, and her camp meeting stories topped mine.

Besides camp meeting, youth camp and boys' and girls' camp were big weeks at the campground. My dad served as a camp counselor many times over the years. The position had little to do with counseling and much to do with crowd control: getting kids to meals and services on time, keeping them within the boundaries of the campground, and getting the boys to bed and quiet by lights out.

After that, the fun began for the counselors. Those who didn't have to stay in the dorms with the kids met in the dining hall. Obviously, all of the adults couldn't leave the kids in the dorms, so they traded nights to go or stay.

During one of his stints as a counselor at boys' and girls' camp, my dad got to have his turn in the dining hall after the kids had gone to bed. He stayed until midnight, playing *Sorry!* and *Monopoly*, telling jokes, eating popcorn, and cutting up with the other counselors.

When he got back to the dorm, all was quiet. The boys were all asleep, so he slipped into his bed as quietly as possible. Halfway in, he realized he was not alone under the sheet. A cold and clammy four-foot long snake was stretched out down the middle of the bed. Holding in a shriek so that he didn't wake up the kids, he made quick work of getting out of his bed. Grabbing his flashlight to get a better look, he realized the snake was as dead as a seminary chapel service. That changed everything. This was a prank, and it wasn't going to end with him.

He was staying on the second floor of the dorm, and one stairway was the only way to get to the bathroom or out of the building. The top step became the rattlesnake's new resting place. My dad could go to sleep in almost any situation, so he got back in his bed—minus the snake—and started sawing logs.

He woke to a boy's shrill scream around 3:00 a.m. A dozen or so boys and my dad rolled from their bunks and scrambled to the commotion. The boys all got a good laugh even though their prank had come back on them. My dad just smiled and went back to bed.

The next morning, the second-floor boys dragged into breakfast looking a little rough, but that was okay. They had another good camp story to tell.

Some churches have given up on having a campground; they are expensive to maintain, and lifestyles have changed. Sports and music have become so demanding that kids don't have time to go to camp, and that's a shame. For spiritual growth and just good fun, nothing beats spending a week of each summer at church camp. Those times still strengthen me and make me smile. I'm glad I got to go.

REENACTMENT

Sundays were the biggest day of the week for us; they were my favorite for both spiritual and social reasons. We always got to the church sometime after nine, depending on how long it took my mom to get the potatoes and carrots peeled, the roast started, the kids spiffed up, and the Sunday school lesson finalized.

Daddy went to the church early to prepare and pray. Since my mother didn't get a driver's license until I was in high school, it was up to my brother to drive us—my mom, my sister, and me—to church. We got into his 1963 Chevy Impala, went three blocks east on Cottonwood in Ardmore, Oklahoma, and arrived at our home away from home.

Sunday school started at 9:30 a.m. I was in the third grade, so first I headed to the primary and junior department "opening exercises," which did not include calisthenics, but did include prayer and the singing of excellent songs such as "The B-I-B-L-E," "Climb, Climb Up Sunshine Mountain" complete with motions, and "Jesus Loves Me."

Next, we went to Sunday school class. Following the lesson, a short break gave people time to make their way to the sanctuary for the worship service.

My mother sat on the left side of the sanctuary in the third row from the front, toward the middle of the pew. I sat with her. I was not allowed to bring coloring books and toys to church. I did make good use of the tithing envelopes, filling in all of the closed letters that were printed on the envelope. I could only get by with using one per service. I dug bobby pins out of mother's purse, and these became slender bobby pin people, and their world was the top of the hymnal on my lap.

If the sermon went on very long, I would switch to playing with a pretty handkerchief, which was also in my mom's purse. I would fold the handkerchief in half diagonally, roll up both ends until they met in the center, and then pull one layer of the bottom back up over the top. This left me with twin babies in a cradle. I rocked them by holding the corners of the handkerchief.

The service began at 10:30 a.m. Opening prayer was followed by Dr. Mac leading the congregational singing: "Victory in Jesus," "Every Day with Jesus," and "He is Able to Deliver Thee."

The announcements and the offering were topped off by Chick Mason singing "Fill My Cup, Lord," and then Daddy got up to preach. He was a good preacher; he read the scripture with familiarity and ease, illustrated his points with stories of his childhood in western Oklahoma, and often quoted poems. Best of all, he knew the Savior in a way that made others want to know Him too.

I was listening to the sermon and playing with my bobby pin people when Margaret Marlor, the church pianist, stole my attention. She was sitting in a pew in front of us and a little to the left. The contortions she went into were inexplicable. Had she been stricken with sudden, violent illness? Was she choking on a peppermint? I was fixated. Mother, undoubtedly, wondered if she should go to Margaret's side and check on her.

We had been watching her for a few seconds when distraction number two commanded our utmost attention. Who cared about Margaret Marlor now? We had problems of our own. A snake was slithering toward us underneath the pews. We had just sung "He Is Able to Deliver Thee," so I should have known I would be okay, but I wasn't thinking of the song just then. I pulled my feet up onto the pew and tried not to squeal or shriek. My mother maintained her composure with effort, lifting her feet too. Mr. Snake slithered past in his serpentine way, headed toward the slackers in the back.

My dad, meanwhile, was on his third point and was heading toward the conclusion. That worked out well. As he wrapped up the sermon, Daddy could tell that something was wrong on the piano side of the congregation, but he didn't know what it was.

From the pulpit he was aware that a strange effect had started in the front—Margaret Marlor was as white as a sheet—and rippled to pew after pew: Women gasped, children whimpered, men fidgeted.

After the closing prayer, a man in cowboy boots made quick work of crushing the snake's head. Most of the congregation members stopped to get a better look at the intruder as they filed out. Somebody said it was a copperhead. The defeat of the serpent in the house of worship seemed symbolically appropriate, a small-scale reenactment of a much bigger story.

SHOES

Lola Getchell is one of the faithful. She is a humble lady who taught a first and second-grade-boys' Sunday school class for twenty years. At eight-five, she has slowed down some, but for fifty years or so, Lola took part in every church event: pitch-in dinners, revivals, prayer meetings, and baby showers. Her husband, Don, never came to church. My dad, interested in seeing him come to Christ, visited at their home one evening. When it was time to go, my dad said, "Don, I sure would like to see you come to church with Lola."

"Reverend Johnson, I'm just not much of a churchgoing man. I don't even own a pair of shoes that would be fit to wear to church," Don confessed.

"What size do you wear?" my dad asked.

"Ten."

"That's what size I wear," Dad said as he bent down, untied his shoes, and took them off. "Here, try these on. How do they fit?"

Surprised to see the reverend in sock feet in his living room, Don put them on. "About right," he said.

"I have an extra pair of dress shoes I never wear. I'll bring them by for you." My dad put his shoes back on, had prayer with the Getchells, and drove home. The next day, he left a pair of brown wingtips on the Getchells' front porch.

Don began to come to church with Lola shortly after that. Eventually, he accepted the salvation that Christ freely gives. He wore those shoes to church for years. Since then, he has gone on to heaven. Who knew a pair of shoes could make such a difference?

THE BENEFITS OF BEING DRAGGED TO CHURCH EVERY TIME THE DOORS WERE OPEN

I attended a myriad of services growing up: Sunday school and Sunday morning worship; Sunday night evangelistic services; Wednesday night prayer meetings; revivals twice a year (Tuesday through Sunday nights); zone rallies; a week of indoor camp meetings in January; a week of camp meetings at the church campground in July, a week of youth camp, and a week of Vacation Bible School each summer; sunrise services on Easter, watch night services to pray in the new year, and special services in between. I learned a lot in church.

World geography and cultures—Missionaries from all over the globe came to speak at our church. They showed slides, talked about black mambas, wore strange clothing, and displayed artifacts from their countries. They read scripture in other languages. Listening to them, I understood that I was part of something bigger than myself.

Travel—Church conventions took me to destinations I might not have reached otherwise: Miami, Dallas, Kansas City, Estes Park, and Los Angeles. I always made new friends. While traveling, my family and I would attend church and felt welcomed wherever we went.

Music—Most of the churches I went to had a choir, some had an orchestra, and all of them had people singing "specials," often preceded by a testimony that ended with "Pray for me as I sing. I haven't had time to practice." We had a yearly cantata, a children's choir, a teen choir, and a traveling youth choir called the Impact Team. We learned to sight read, harmonize, and watch the director.

Crafts—Vacation Bible School involved some pretty impressive and complicated crafts. Different colored seeds glued to a piece of plywood became a rooster that is still framed and hangs in my mom's garage. She can't throw it away because my brother made it in Vacation Bible School as a child, carefully adding seeds each of the six days of VBS. I look at that rooster and wonder how the VBS teachers ever got the children to do all that, especially before Adderall.

Activities—Going to youth camp, hiking in state parks, canoeing, sledding, and ice skating: These are things I did with my youth group, and they were a few of my favorites. We were usually transported to and fro in an infamous church bus.

Talent—A yearly talent contest encouraged kids to excel in music, speaking, and art. We competed at local, zone, and district levels, with tougher competition at each level. No one ever expected to beat the Sneed sisters from Shelbyville, who sang as a trio and were just as cute as they were talented.

Public speaking—I grew up hearing evangelists and preachers who had mastered the art of public speaking. I didn't know how good they were until I became an adult and realized not everybody can do that. When I was ten years old, I got a ventriloquist "dummy" for Christmas, and my dad had Tommy and me telling Bible stories to children within a few months. When I was in seventh grade, I upgraded to a professional "figure," and J. P. and I traveled around speaking to churches and civic groups for the next several years. People always liked J. P. better than me, but I'm okay with that.

Listening—Attending three church services every week from birth to adulthood forced me to learn to sit still and listen. My mother also had a hand in that. As a teenager, I found I was less distracted by nice Christian boys in the pew in front of me if I took notes. Quieting myself, taking notes, and listening are disciplines that I still use today.

Reading—The Bible, Sunday school papers, and missionary books all provided reading material. Each year, the church got a different set of missionary books full of faith-building stories from foreign lands. The children had their own set of books, and my parents read them to my sister and me as bedtime stories until we were old enough to read on our own.

Memorization—For Bible quizzing, I memorized dozens of verses each year. Part of my motivation was just to beat the Illinois quiz team, but all that memorizing has worked out well for two reasons: I still have many scriptures in my head and heart, and I still know how to memorize.

Interacting with multiple generations—As a kid at church, I helped with the younger children, enjoyed knowing a whole bunch of elderly folk (some of whom acted like adopted grandparents), and had friends of all ages in between.

Manners and hospitality—My mom and dad taught me that every person who came into the church was someone Jesus died for. If Jesus could do that, I could at least be friendly. Most Sundays a different family was sitting around our dining room table eating roast and potatoes with us after the morning service, or coming over after the Sunday evening service for popcorn and a game of *Sorry!* From a young age, I had table manners and conversation skills, even though sometimes I forgot where I had put them.

Robert's Rules of Order—Conventions and assembly meetings were conducted in an orderly fashion. Thus, I learned what it means to "call for the previous question" and have a quorum. Sometimes my dad would come home from a church board meeting and grin as he told us the board meeting attendance was down, but enough people showed up to "have a quarrel."

Community service—Visiting nursing homes, making hospital calls, and taking food to the poor were part of my life before community service and volunteerism became cool. My dad's calling was to care for the flock, and sometimes he let me tag along.

Money management—Throughout most of my childhood, my weekly allowance was a quarter. This meant my tithe every week was two-and-a-half cents. I rounded up to three, put it in a tithe envelope, and figured out how to make the other eighty-eight percent do what it needed to do. Taking out the tithe first has been my policy throughout life, even when money was tight. What a great investment!

Recipes—We didn't need recipes.com or the food channel. At church pitch-ins we found out who made the best sugar cream pie (which is mixed on the stove and then baked), corn casserole (best if made with Indiana corn), or sweet potato casserole (good enough to make you slap your grandma) and then got the recipe by looking at whose name was taped to the dish.

College visits—Every year, someone from the church would take a group of young people to Illinois for a visit to Olivet Nazarene University. Over the years, dozens of kids from our church ended up graduating from Olivet and taking their Christian worldview into their spheres of influence. The ripple effect of those college visits is immeasurable.

Of course, this is only a partial list of fringe benefits. No organization I know can match the benefits of growing up in a church, surrounded by people who love each other. The Boy Scouts are remarkable, and public schools might come close, but the church is unparalleled by any earthly institution because of the spiritual truths it offers.

The church points me to Jesus, who shows me the way to live, what living really means, and how to finish well. I recommend it.

ROCKING CHAIR THERAPY

A baby cried, and someone immediately went to pick him up and give him his pacifier. The smells of Wet Wipes, Johnson's baby powder, and the dirty diaper pail competed in the background. I was holding my son, Gus, and feeding him Cheerios one at a time. I would put him down if another baby needed attention; it was my Sunday of the month. Any church lady with an ounce of volunteerism has probably "walked a mile in my moccasins." We had to take our shoes off for the job, so it might be more appropriate to say "rocked a while in my sock feet."

Our church nursery had two types of volunteers. Moms like me rotated in and out of duty on a monthly schedule. We put in our time because we were needed and we recognized that it was only fair to take turns. The rotating moms were of little real significance to the nursery operations compared to the other type of volunteer.

Two grandmotherly ladies, Mabel and Betty, went to the basement instead of the sanctuary every Sunday. They were not waiting for a Sunday off. Those two were in the nursery every Sunday I took my children there, which probably covered a span of four years.

When my kids had grown up and gone off to college, Mabel and Betty were still in the nursery. Mabel couldn't get up and down to pick up the babies, but she could sit in a rocking chair and hold them. She knew how to calm a crying baby. Mabel was forced to retire after forty-eight years of nursery duty; she couldn't get up and down the steps to the nursery.

Betty eventually had to give it up because of her husband's health. By the time they retired from the nursery, Mabel and Betty had seen the bare bottoms of most of the people who grew up in our church, some of them forty-something-year-old men now. Mabel and Betty were an excellent pair of volunteers, and they offered more than childcare.

My children weren't the only ones who needed care by the time our young family got to the church on Sunday mornings. Mabel and Betty must have had secret radar that detected frazzled moms. Undoubtedly, all of their internal alarms went off when I opened the nursery room door most Sundays. Sometimes they put the baby in the "punkin seat" down in a safe place and held me, instead, in a grandmotherly hug.

Neither of them had been trained as counselors, but many young mothers had therapy sessions with them. Mabel and Betty didn't throw pity parties in the nursery, and husband bashing couldn't even get a good start with those two. They were advocates of "Keep calm and carry on" before it became a trendy saying. They talked a lot about prayer and trusting God and how everything would work out.

One Sunday I sat in the rocking chair next to Mabel venting about how much I had to do and how crazy my week had been. Fishing for a little sympathy, I told her about Tuesday: I had worked all day, graded papers, fixed supper, and then gone to town for choir practice while Mark watched the kids. The best and finishing line of my sob story detailed how the dirty supper dishes were still on the table when I got home from choir practice. In a thinly masked effort to get Mabel to say Mark should have done the dishes, I said, "I don't know why I thought the dishes would be done when I got home. I guess I was hoping an angel would just show up in the kitchen and do the dishes, but . . . "

Mabel had heard enough. She gently interrupted me with her slow Kentucky drawl. "Honey, let me tell you something I learned a long time ago. You're the angel."

Proverbs 25:11 says, "A word fitly spoken is like apples of gold in settings of silver." I don't know much about gold apples, but I'm pretty sure Mabel's line was one, and she's been saying it in my head over the years. When I'm tempted to throw myself a pity party or blame somebody else for life's inconveniences, I hear Mabel saying, "You're the angel," and carry on.

SIXTIETH ANNIVERSARY

A sixtieth wedding anniversary is remarkable: It speaks of strength in a relationship as well as self-control and perseverance in two individuals. Our sweet friends John and Betty Thurston celebrated their sixtieth and have added eight more.

Betty was one of the nursery ladies who took care of our babies at church. Later, when the kids were old enough to sit through the services, they would find Betty before church and give her a hug. She would give them gum. John played bass with Mark in the worship band on Sunday nights. John and Betty made church feel like family.

On the day of their sixtieth anniversary celebration at the church, Mark couldn't go, but I went anyway to honor the Thurstons. The event was from two to four in the afternoon, and guests could drop in and leave when they wanted.

When I arrived, I signed the guest book and put my card in the basket. The room was crowded. John and Betty were surrounded by friends, and it soon became obvious to me that I wouldn't get to talk to them in the amount of time I had. That was okay; I knew I would see them next Sunday at church. After visiting with a few people, I made my way toward the door.

As I walked out of the room to leave, I was surprised to see Betty! The two of us stood in the hallway by ourselves and exchanged a hug. "Getting to your sixtieth anniversary is quite an accomplishment!" I said. "Congratulations! I'm pretty sure Mark and I won't reach our sixtieth."

Betty kept an arm around me as she softly said, "Honey, don't give up on your marriage. You can make it. God will help you."

Laughing, I explained, "Oh, no, we're getting along fine. It's just that we got a late start on our marriage. I don't think Mark will live that long."

I reminded Mark of that story a few days ago. We laughed about it again, and then he did some math, taking issue with what I had told Betty.

"I think I can make it; I don't see why not. I'll only be ninety-four."

I agreed with him and retracted my dismal prediction. We're still getting along fine, and we're almost halfway to our sixtieth. The first twenty years were the hardest.

Betty was right: God has helped us this far. A sixtieth anniversary celebration sounds good to us. We're still working out the details, but we have some time.

HEAVEN

My daddy was a pastor for forty years. In retirement, he filled in for ministers who went on vacation and for churches that were between pastors. In 2010 he was diagnosed with pancreatic cancer. Just a few days after his diagnosis, Margaret and I went to Oklahoma expecting to visit him in the hospital. We had no idea we were also making the trip for his funeral. I am thankful that we got to Oklahoma City in time to talk to him for a couple of days before he (as I heard him often say at funerals) left this world and entered the next. On the day of the funeral, as I was getting ready to go to the church, I opened a desk drawer in my mom and dad's office. Neatly stacked sermon outlines brought tears to my eyes. He had boxes of them in the closet, but the outline at the top of the stack I "happened" to come across in the desk that day was a sermon on heaven. Here it is, modified for readability.

Introduction: I studied about the state of Indiana as a boy in a country school on the sun-scorched plains of western Oklahoma. I never dreamed of going there, for it was a land far away that had no particular appeal to me.

World War II came on. Friends moved to Indiana to work in defense plants. Boys were in the service there. They began to write back and tell what a beautiful country it was. My brother went and came back in a few years and told about the good jobs. These things began to interest me. I got an old geography book and looked at the block named Indiana on the map.

One summer (sixteen years old) I decided to go. I went to the bus station and got the price of the ticket and a map of the roads we would take. I studied the map and roads until I knew almost every town between Indiana and Oklahoma. I got together the money, bought a ticket, and boarded the bus. I rode through the hot, dusty endless plains clear across Oklahoma. That night we were going through the Ozark mountains when I fell asleep. The next morning, I woke up in a beautiful country of green fields, rolling hills, and orchards such as I had never seen.

A. When I was a child, I heard Mother talk about heaven. Often she sang,

"O think of the home over there
  By the side of the river of light,
  Where the saints all immortal and fair,
  Are robed in their garments of white."

That, too, was a land far away, and I did not think much about it as a boy. As I grew older, neighbors and loved ones began to move to that country, so I became interested. I got the old Bible and traced the route. I made inquiry as to the conditions for passage to heaven. As I studied the land beyond the blue, my desire increased.

One night at a mourner's bench, I bought my ticket. Now I am on my way. At times it has tunnels, darkness, barren plains, mountains. I know that someday I will fall asleep while crossing the desert of life, but will awake to find the plains gone, and I will roll across the hills of glory. Then I will know the truth of the song "The toils of the road will seem nothing when I get to the end of the way."

B. We are interested in our homes here. Why not our eternal homes? No one can give better reasons for their interest in earthly cities than a Christian can for the heavenly city. Abraham was so interested in heaven that he never built a home. "He waited for the city which has foundations, whose builder and maker is God."

C. Heaven is a place. Jesus said, "Let not your heart be troubled. . . . I go to prepare a place for you." Heaven is a place just like Hope, Arkansas, is a place.

D. Heaven is a prepared place. "I go to prepare a place for you." I like the personal note (you).

Illustration: A mother in San Francisco said to Brother Mitchell, "Do you think I will know my son John?"

Bro. Mitchell: Would you be satisfied if you didn't?

The mother: (tears in her eyes) No, I wouldn't.

Bro. Mitchell: If it takes that to satisfy you, you will know him.

Made to measure, like a tailor-made suit. No two alike, like fingerprints. Heaven will be made to suit you. What would satisfy me wouldn't satisfy you.

E. Father encourages. While Jesus is preparing us a place, the Holy Spirit is preparing us for that place. God the Father encourages us.

F. Heaven is a happy place. "Let not your heart be troubled. . . . " We like to think of home as a place where trouble never comes. Trouble, sickness, death, sorrow, and all barriers will be gone.

G. Place of rest. Rest is unknown to some.

H. Gregory and Margaret—Because of his love for Margaret, he was banished from homeland. Before leaving, he told her not to cry, but to bring a lantern each night to the shore on the high rocks overlooking the water. "I will come back when I find us a home." People made fun of her, talked about her. One night on the shore, she heard her name, "Margaret." She shouted "Gregory!" and ran to the water's edge to meet him. They sailed away to their new home.

Conclusion: Because our Lord loved this world, many tried to banish Him from it. Before He went away, He called a few of those who loved Him aside and said, "Let not your heart be troubled. . . . " In other words, watch and wait. If we are loyal, loved ones may drive some of us from home. We may be called strangers and fools, but if we stay near the shore and keep our lamps trimmed and burning, one of these days we will hear the splash of a boatman's oar, and see the old ship of Zion coming around the bend. Our names will be called; we will throw our grip on board and sail away.

PARABLE OF A PIG
AND A PASTOR

Almost any preschooler would like to pet a real-live pig. Dave Graham, the maintenance man for our church and daycare, had recently acquired one. Knowing how much the children would enjoy seeing it, Dave arranged to bring the pig to daycare. Only about ten weeks old—still considered a piglet— he was about the size of a cocker spaniel. In pig years, Wilbert was a preschooler. Wee children and a wee pig seemed like a winning combination, so Dave crated Wilbert, put him in his pickup, and off they went to the daycare.

The teachers had talked up the pig for days in advance. Knowing how excited the kids would be to see Wilbert, they went over proper pig protocol: Don't try to pick up the pig, don't ride the pig, don't kiss the pig, don't scare the pig. Excitement had been building, and the children were so ready to meet Wilbert.

Nobody had counted on how excited Wilbert would become when he saw the children, all sixty-five of them, waiting for him on the school playground. The children screamed with delight when they got their first glimpse of him. Then they crowded in: Dozens of hands reached toward him, pushing, pulling, petting, pinching.

Wilbert was way out of his comfort zone, and soon he'd had enough. Sensing that whoever was at the other end of his leash had momentarily lost hold, he made a break for it. He had navigated through skinned knees, smelly socks, and tennis shoes and was in open country before the children even had time to realize their show of friendship had been rejected. Sometimes relationships work out that way, but preschool is probably too early for that lesson. They'll get it soon enough.

Two sides of the playground are enclosed by the building. The other two sides are flanked by recently planted cornfields. Nobody had made a contingency plan for what to do if the pig got loose in the unfenced playground. Wilbert had made his move suddenly, so that gave him a big head start. He was covering territory while everybody else was trying to figure out what to do.

Dave wasn't a "spring chicken" anymore, that's for sure, so he wasn't going to chase a pig. Of course the children were up for the chase but were forbidden to go after him. The teachers gave each other stunned looks above the heads of their young charges, trying to figure out who should stay with the children and who should chase the pig. Some of the younger teachers took off after Wilbert.

Miss Sue, who is in charge of the daycare cafeteria, had watched the whole episode through the back screen door of the kitchen. Knowing she couldn't do anything to help,

Sue turned away from the door to get back to making chili. Just then, Pastor Jim breezed into the kitchen for his customary morning greetings and donut from our local Jack's Donuts shop.

"Good morning, Sue! How's it going?" Jim asked, smiling.

"Well, not that great. Dave Graham's pig just got away from them on the playground."

"What?"

"Just look for yourself. He's gotten loose and nobody can catch him."

Pastor Jim looked out the screen, saw the need, and shot out the door to help. Doesn't everybody want a pastor like that? Even though Jim is forty years old and not a fitness fanatic, he's still in better shape than many his age or younger. Digging deep and reconnecting with his former high school basketball player self, he sprinted across the playground.

Unfortunately, he was running with handicaps: a dress shirt and a tie, khakis, and dress shoes. Furthermore, it had rained for the last five days, so as soon as he got off the pavement and into the grass, he was in squishy ground. Where the cornfield began, the squish turned to mud.

Who knows what goes through the mind of a forty-year-old pastor chasing a pig through the mud while a daycare population looks on? Perhaps *They never warned me about stuff like this in Bible college.* Maybe *I've made up my mind. I am going to ask the church council for that raise.* Possibly the scripture: *Run with endurance the race that is set before us.* Whatever it was, adrenalin kicked in, and he focused on the pig.

Nobody knew a pig—especially a little guy with such short, stubby legs—could run so fast. Wilbert was "picking them up and setting them down" so fast his hind feet were almost running over his front feet. As the distance between the pursuing teachers and Wilbert got farther and farther, it became obvious that Pastor Jim was their only hope. Jim was running out of breath, but knew he had to keep going. Between the pig and the pastor, mud was flying everywhere.

Finally, Jim got close enough to Wilbert that he thought he could grab the leash if he dove for it, so he did. Pete Rose would have been proud. Firmly grasping the end of the leash, Jim slid to a stop, and so did the pig. The second it became clear that Pastor Jim had caught Wilbert, sixty-five preschoolers and one pig squealed.

Jim found himself lying in the mud just trying to breathe. He was sweaty and spent, and the cool mud actually felt good to him. He held onto the leash and rested. Finally, one of the teachers caught up with him and said, "Pastor Jim, aren't you going to get up?"

The next Sunday at church, Jim worked the great pig chase into his sermon. His closing point was that in the midst of life we all have times when we're running hard, doing good, and helping others, but find ourselves exhausted and lying in the mud. We have a choice: We can either stay in the mud and get used to it, or with God's help, get up, wash the mud off, and keep going.

Farmhouse

FARMHOUSE

I saiah and Susannah Ellabarger built their house in 1879. This fact is etched in stone on a plaque they placed by the front door when they built it. The 1879 construction was actually added to an older house, which was built sometime in the 1850s.

The original structure has a fireplace that is five-and-a-half feet wide and four feet tall. A well-used bread oven is nestled in the wall beside it. We still have the hook that held the pots above the fire.

The house sits on an old road, a winding, curvy road that goes from one destination to the next, regardless of the neatly numbered roads it intersects. The land the house sits on was first deeded in 1825. A lot of struggle and resourcefulness and love and hope and pain and perseverance and death and birth and hard work happened here before I arrived, and I respect that. Mark grew up here, and this is where I've lived longer than anyplace else; it feels like home to us. It is a good place.

In addition to its history, our house could be set apart from others by what it doesn't have. We have a basement, but most of it only has a dirt floor. We don't have central air. Mark thinks that's what our tall windows are for, and he prefers the climate nature brings (except in the winter, of course). The furnace only heats the first floor, not the upstairs, because heat rises. Not enough heat rises for me on cold winter nights.

We got rid of the television years ago because we didn't have the extra time or brain cells. When the kids were in high school, we talked about getting one, but they said "Nah."

Before we start sounding like minimalists, here's some of what we do have. A big barn with a loft is hard to beat for fun. For most of the summer, the kids built tunnels and forts out of bales of straw and swung from ropes that hung from the rafters, just as their dad did thirty-five years earlier.

Some years we had a corn maze. Groups of kids from the church would come out for a hayride and weenie roast around a campfire and get lost in the corn.

Some of our entertainment was not for the faint of heart. We had a zip line running from a barn window to a big branch of the huge maple tree that stood in the front yard. Another pastime for our kids and their friends was climbing the Harvestore. Gus and his friends figured out how to get pumpkins to the top so that they could drop them and watch them splatter.

We also had movies on the barn wall for the youth group. A lawn chair, a blanket, a hot chocolate, a starry night, and a movie on the barn wall always add up to a good time.

Since we live in Indiana, we had to have a basketball goal. Both of our kids played some ball. When Mark got a new cement floor for the barn, a basketball goal had to be included. As long as daylight lasted, the kids jumped on the trampoline, played volleyball, and ushered in twilight with their favorite, ultimate Frisbee. When the sun went down, they switched from Frisbee to Capture the Flag or headed to the barn, moved the farm equipment out, and played pickup basketball until curfew called the game.

One of the highlights of our summer is the annual hog roast. Around two hundred people usually show up, some of whom we don't even know. Our friends bring their friends, and everybody brings a covered dish. We eat and talk and play corn hole and have three-legged races with varying categories of competitors: father-son, mother-daughter, siblings, couples, under ten, and over sixty. A lot of people just watch because it's more fun to watch their friends fall and get all tangled up with each other than it is to risk the embarrassment. Nobody's thinking about life's problems while watching or participating in the three-legged race. For laughter and therapy, it's the best.

Over the years, we have had many guests. Some stayed for a meal or an evening, some stayed overnight, some stayed for a few weeks, and some stayed for months. Many have said, "I can't remember when I got such a good night's sleep."

One of Gus's second-grade buddies, Todd, used to come to our house and play. His mother told me that one day he came home with a picture he had drawn at school. Todd explained that his teacher had asked the kids to draw a picture of their favorite place. Most of the kids drew a beach or a zoo or Disney World. Todd drew Gus's house. I was honored, and I like to think God was too.

When Mark and I were married, my dad prayed that our home would be a foretaste of heaven. That's what we want, and I'm thankful that others seem to get an extra dose of peace and joy when they are here. When Gus was a little guy saying his bedtime prayers, he used to say, "Thank you, God, for putting us in this place where we like it." Amen, and thanks to the Ellabargers for building a good house.

COUNTRY ROADS

The roads in our part of the county are potholed from seasons of freezing and thawing and semi-trucks overflowing with grain. They're grooved by Amish buggy wheels and muddied by tractors and wagons pulling out of the fields. They're dangerous in the mornings and evenings, not because of traffic, but because deer seldom look both ways before they cross. These same roads are where the dogs and I go for walks; I watch the sunset while they patrol the fields and side ditches, guarding their galaxy from outlaw possums and rabbits.

The side ditches are country parking spaces for vehicles of all kinds. In the fall, they are where Mark leaves his trucks to fill with grain when he's harvesting. In the spring, when he's planting, he keeps a pickup truck waiting in the side ditch so that he can go after seed or parts if he needs to. When he's done with a field, he usually drives the tractor home and then somebody takes him back to get his truck. If he finishes at night and is really tired, he might leave the truck on the roadside until the next day.

We had a '73 Mercedes diesel that Mark loved. The oil plug fell out of it on our honeymoon, but that's a tale for another time. Despite that, we still loved each other and the car. We used the car for years as a cool, quaint vehicle until the cool factor was eclipsed by frequent trips to see Fritz, the Mercedes mechanic. Eventually, I gave up driving the car, but Mark knows enough about how to tinker with mechanical problems that he kept our old friend going, finally using it as a farm vehicle.

One evening during the height of planting season, a dust-covered Mark came in the house with a puzzled look on his face.

"Have you seen the Mercedes lately?" According to the Indiana Farm Bureau, an Indiana farmer feeds an average of one hundred fifty-five people. Mark had been planting like a madman for days, forfeiting sleep, regular meals, and other frivolities to take responsibility for feeding his one hundred fifty-five. In the middle of this farming frenzy, it occurred to Mark that he had lost a car.

"No, I haven't seen it. Do you need it?"

"I have my truck, but I would like to know where the Mercedes is." As Mark threw together a sandwich and I filled his Thermos with lemonade to take, we figured out that neither of us had seen the Mercedes for days. I suggested it might be at his parents' house across the field, but he had already checked there and at his sister's house down the road.

"When was the last time you had it?" I reverted to the question we all ask when we are looking for that which is lost. Thinking back took Mark down several country roads and several days into the past. He had finished a field late one night and had driven the tractor and planter home.

Following that lead, Mark and I got in the truck and we went to that field to look for the Mercedes. There it was, bless its heart, sitting in the side ditch five miles from home. What once was lost had now been found, keys in the ignition and the windows down. Mark dropped me off and went back to the field he was planting. I drove the car home, enjoying the cool of the evening and grateful for our farming community, side ditches, and country roads.

GOOD NEIGHBORS

Over the years, Mark has hired a variety of guys to help him on the farm. Good help is hard to find, but we have been blessed with some good workers. One of the really good ones was Zach, who worked for us during high school and after he graduated. He was a tall, lanky, quiet boy who paid attention to what he was doing, which is very important in farming, and enjoyed working as much as he enjoyed anything.

One spring, Mark sent Zach to plow a field about six miles from our house. They hooked the plow up to the tractor, and Zach moseyed through the country roads until he finally got to Last Mile Road and the field he needed to work. He had been plowing for a few hours, enjoying the thrill of the chase from one end of the field to the next, when the tractor began to have mechanical problems. Zach was smart enough to know when to stop in order to prevent further damage.

His problem then became how to get back to our farm. This was before cell phones were in everybody's pocket. The house at the corner of the field looked like his best option. It was a little bit of a walk just to get from the tractor to the house. A middle-aged man answered Zach's knock on the door.

"Sorry to bother you, but I've been plowing this field and the tractor broke down. Would you mind letting me use your phone to try to call the guy I work for?"

"Who do you work for?"

"Mark Goggin. He rents this field. I don't know if I can get anybody to answer the phone or not. He's probably not in the house, but I might as well try."

"Just take my truck," the man offered. "The keys are in it. I have to go someplace, but you can just bring it back and leave the keys in it."

"Thanks! I appreciate it," Zach said. He walked to the truck, wiped his boots off in the grass, got in, and drove away.

When he got back to our farm, Zach didn't find Mark in the barn, so he came to the house to see if I knew where he was. He told me about the tractor and how Mark's friend had let him borrow the truck. I helped Zach find Mark, and they gathered some tools and headed back to the field, Zach in the borrowed pickup followed by Mark in our truck.

That night after the sun went down and Mark finally came into the house, we talked about the day. I mentioned how nice it was of his friend to let Zach borrow the truck.

"I don't know the guy," Mark said.

"Really? Zach and I assumed he was your friend since he offered to let Zach borrow the truck when he said he worked for you."

"Nope, I've never met him. I guess he figured Zach's story was believable. He must be a nice guy."

That's the kind of thing that happens where I live.

DUCK BOOTS

At the age of four, our daughter, Christina, lived in a state of almost uninterrupted bliss. Her biggest problem on a typical day was having to drink juice out of the wrong-colored cup. Worries were unheard of. The day that later became known as the "duck boots day" promised to be an excellent one as Christina got up and got dressed. Gus and I were going to be away most of the day, and Christina knew she was going to spend a big part of the day "helping" her dad on the farm.

She hurriedly dressed in her overalls and then struggled and fought her way into her very special boots. These rubber duck boots were white above the ankles, but yellow on the part that covered the feet, forming duck bills. The duck eyes were toward the top of the feet. They were one excellent pair of boots, and Christina was always proud when she wore them. One last tug made her apparel complete, with some of her favorite things in the whole world right on her feet. She jumped up, confident and ready to go.

She followed her dad across the yard and driveway to the cattle lot, listening to their moos. They seemed to be saying, "Hurry up!" As Mark fed the cattle, Christina climbed unsteadily onto the rusty gates to watch the cattle eat. They shoved each other impatiently for a chance at a mouthful of silage.

Soon her attention began to wander, and the cows were not so interesting. She remembered that she was supposed to be helping Dad, so she climbed off the gate to go find him. She could go fast in her duck boots, and she ran onward to her mission. She zoomed past gates and sheds and then skirted the manure pit, but not by far enough.

As she took a step, the rubber heel of her beautiful duck boot plopped into a mucky mixture that brought her to a dead halt. Upset at the thought of losing her wonderful boot, she strained and pulled frantically, but the boot was being suctioned farther down with each panicked effort from her four-year-old legs. Calling her dad was no use because the feeding machine was too loud. Christina was stuck. She made one last effort to free her boot from the nasty, sticky muck, but instead she slipped and did a perfect belly smack into the manure. Now she was in trouble. The quicksand-like concoction sucked her down, and she could not breathe or make a noise as she sank steadily lower.

Christina was sure her time was up. Her short years of childhood were flashing before her manure-covered eyes when she felt a large, strong hand grabbing the back of her overalls and pulling her away from the monstrous manure. She made vain attempts to wipe off the substance that covered every inch of her but was too terrified and limp to do anything.

Her rescuer, her knight in dirty Carharts, her dad carried her pitiful form over to the hose, where she was mercifully and unmercifully sprayed down. Over and over, the bombardment of icy water shocked her small, shivering, overalls-clad body, but just then anything was better than reeking manure.

On that day, Christina learned that the world is a dangerous place, that she should always be careful, and that she should never get too close to the manure pit.

She also learned that her dad would always have her back. She has kept these lessons throughout her life. The duck boots survived and also seemed to have learned a lesson. They were eventually passed on to Christina's brother, Gus, who wore them proudly around the barn lot. He never had any problems with manure.

OWL

One day long ago when the kids were still in daycare, I had to drive Mark's pickup to school for some reason. I loaded up Christina and Gus and all of our daily baggage and we headed to town in Mark's dusty truck.

The first stop was dropping the kids off at daycare at the church. I slid out of the truck and then unbuckled Gus and told him to come out my side. As he maneuvered himself under the steering wheel, he looked down at his feet and said, "Mommy, why is there an owl in the truck?" I thought he was confused, but after a quick glance under the seat, I was confused. An owl was lying on the floor.

I'm not given to panic attacks, but that would have been a good time for one. My long skirt had been resting on an owl as I drove to town. My common sense told me the owl must be dead, but I'm a "What if?" person. Owls are nocturnal; it was daytime. What if the owl was only napping? It could awake and attack at any minute.

Trying to keep my cool, I shut the door and raced to the other side of the cab to get Christina out. I had no explanation to offer Gus in answer to his question. I checked the kids into daycare and then went to the church office.

A church office is solicited for all kinds of help, but undoubtedly this was the only time they had a request like mine. I asked if anybody could get an owl out of the truck for me. Reverend Gourtney got a pair of gloves and walked with me to the truck. He picked up the owl, confirmed it would never hoot again, and laid it to rest in the back of the truck. I thanked him and went on to school, hoping the excitement of my day would taper off.

That evening Mark gave me a simple explanation. He had hit an owl while he was driving the truck, and it was stuck in the grill when he arrived at his destination. He thought the kids would like to see it, so he had put it in the truck. Then he forgot about it. That explanation made sense coming from a man who is usually thoughtful and sometimes forgetful. We were in Mark's pickup, and in the farmer's territory, who knows what might happen? Who? Who?

BATS

A bat in the house can change the course of a night. Since I am a light sleeper, I am usually the first to know. I hear a bat squeaking or see a bat flitting around the bedroom in the light that comes through the window. I pull the blankets over my head and kick Mark, hoping he will hear my urgent but muffled, "There's a bat in the house!" This part of the script is always the same.

"Hon, there's not a bat in the house. You're having a dream. Go back to sleep." This is followed by more kicking and more muffled insistence. Mark stirs a little bit and again tells me I'm dreaming as I beg him to look for the bat so I won't smother.

Eventually, Mark gets up to appease me and chase the phantom bat that is not in the house. He hasn't been able to hear high-pitched bat noises for several years, so that's no help at all. By this time the bat has flown to the far reaches of the house. Mark always makes the perfectly logical point that he can't catch a bat if he can't find it.

The next step is for him to investigate the bathroom so that he can give me the all-clear to run there with a blanket over my head. That is my safe room, from which I listen intently to bat proceedings. Mark gets the bat-whacking tennis racquet out from under the bed and starts looking behind curtains and turning on all the lights so that we can go back to bed.

Sometimes the search would wake the kids, and they would venture out of bed to join the hunt, tennis racquets in hand. Sometimes even the dog would hear the bat and give a clue by tilting his head while looking very focused. On the worst nights, after an hour of no bat sightings, Mark would give up. He was usually snoring again by the time I got settled. Those nights it was hard for me to get back to sleep. With the blankets pulled up high and a pillow over my head, I would dream of hairnets or rabies.

To Mark's credit, most of the nights we had a bat round-up, he persevered until he found it, hit it with a tennis racquet to stun it, picked it up with a towel, and released it into the night air. I'm not a fan of the catch and release program; I think the same bats come back to their favorite "hangout," but it's been awhile. We've been bat free for a couple of years, so I'm not complaining.

BIRDS

Starlings are clueless enough to meet for conversation and sit on the edge of the stovepipe at the top of our chimney. Perhaps this is the bird version of humans walking around a dormant volcano. This starling gathering occasionally leads to one falling down the stovepipe into the woodstove. The sound of fluttering and flopping in the woodstove is always disturbing to me.

When Mark comes in, my greeting is "There's a bird in the woodstove." Following that announcement, my behavior is predictable; I hide in the bathroom. Mark opens all of the house doors and then opens the woodstove. After the bird emerges from the woodstove and overcomes its confusion, it limps toward the sunshine and an open door, squawking bird curses.

Mark fills the feeders in our yard, and we enjoy seeing nuthatches, finches, doves, sparrows, cardinals, starlings, woodpeckers, robins, and hummingbirds through the kitchen windows. Barn swallows catch mosquitoes for us as we mow the yard, and build their nests of mud in the barn so that we get to see the babies.

One year Mrs. Wren built her nest and hatched her eggs in the hanging flower basket next to the kitchen window. We cohabit peacefully and enjoy each other, especially when the birds stay outside.

MICE AND RATS

Farm life is a life shared with critters. Some are a source of income or pleasure. Others cause grief or anxiety. Mice and rats fit in the latter group.

Mice are a given. We don't have an infestation of mice in the house, but we do have an occasional visitor, especially when the weather gets cold. Their favorite path is along the wall between the oven and the fridge. If I see a mouse, I tell Mark, and we fuss about traps (Mark's choice) versus poison (my choice). Either way, we soon get rid of the rodent.

Our real mouse problems are in farm equipment and our cars, where they go in the winter to be warm. Mice chew on wires in Mark's equipment, wreaking havoc on gauges and electrical systems. They also seem to love our cars. I wish I had a mothball for every time the mechanic at the Toyota dealership carried a very fluffy, disgusting air filter into the waiting area and said, "Ma'am, you have a rodent problem." Nice.

Worst of all, one day Christina was driving down the road when a mouse ran across the dashboard. She pulled over, got out, opened all of the doors, and called her dad. That was one of the few times he ever said to her, "What am I supposed to do? You're on your own, babe."

When we were first married, Mark and I rented a very old house that had started out as a log cabin. It had various haphazard additions, but no design. It had a basement, but no closets. It had a cute little loft bedroom, but no air conditioning. It also had a rat problem.

Sighting a rat in the house raises everything to a level of excitement mice can never touch. Mark brought a bucket of rat poison home and started to go down in the basement to feed the rats, but it was late in the day and he was tired, so he took the lid off of the bucket, set it on the top basement step, and said, "I'll go down there and scatter it tomorrow."

The next morning when he opened the basement door, the D-Con was all gone, saving him the trouble of distribution. It was a good start.

When the kids were in elementary school, we had another memorable moment involving rats. One early spring day we were all working in the barn to get an area ready for the 4-H pigs. As we were moving bales of straw, a rat ran out from under one of them and raced out of the barn, darting toward the house.

Christina, ten or eleven at the time, rocketed after the rat and headed it off. When the rat saw her, he changed his course and looked for greener pastures. I was surprised that she took off after a rat, not sure what she was doing. Was she trying to catch the rat? Kill the rat? What?

When the excitement was over, I asked. She said, "I didn't want the rat to find a way to get into the basement, so I got in front of it to shoo it away." As a human resident in the house, I was glad the rat was redirected. As a mom, I was proud of Christina's spunk. She could have jumped on a straw bale and screamed, but she fixed a problem instead. That's the kind of girl she is.

We'll never be rid of all of the varmints, but living on the farm is so great it far outweighs the aggravation of putting up with these uninvited critters.

---❧❦❧---

DOGS

We are a two-dog family. Two dogs can keep each other company. One usually favors the outdoors and the other likes to be indoors. Twenty-seven years of farm dogs are featured in these interviews.

Name: Brittany
Breed: golden retriever
   How did you get to the farm?
   Mark purchased me when I was a puppy. I knew Mark before he knew Annette.
   What are your strengths?
   I am very patient. When Christina and Gus were toddlers, I would lie down on the floor and let them straddle me. They thought I was just as much fun as a rocking horse, so I did a lot of babysitting. Even though they sometimes pulled my ears, I never nipped or growled.

What are your weaknesses?

I was caught in a barbed-wire fence when I was young. Mark couldn't find me for days. The wire was twisted around my leg, and it cut the circulation off. By the time he found me, they were able to save my life, but not my leg. After the surgery, I couldn't jump in and out of the back of a pickup as most farm dogs like to do, but I still had a good life.

What is your most memorable moment?

My muzzle had turned white with age before arthritis caught up with me. Eventually, I couldn't get up and down to go outside. All I could do was rest on the floor. Mark, who is one quality human being, would pick me up and carry me outside several times a day. A man can be a dog's best friend. Mark was patient with me when I was helpless, so like Charles Dickens, I would say, "It was the best of times, it was the worst of times."

Name: Babs
Breed: Welsh corgi

How did you get to the farm?

My family purchased me when I was a puppy.

What are your strengths?

I am a little dog with a big dog's personality.

What are your weaknesses?

Food is the most important part of my life. Foraging for food is my first priority. I am a butterball.

What is your most memorable moment?

One evening the family had made chocolate chip cookies. They were enjoying warm cookies in the family room and didn't offer me one, so I went to the kitchen.

Somehow—I can't imagine how—the wastebasket got knocked over. I began to sniff a large empty chocolate chip bag for leftover crumbs. To my dismay, the bag got caught on my head. When Gus came back to the kitchen to get a glass of milk, he found me bumping my way around, trying to get the bag off my head. They're still laughing about it.

Name: Sam
Breed: chocolate Labrador mix
How did you get to the farm?

My mother got into some trouble with the neighbor dog. My siblings and I were being given away. Mark heard about it and came and picked me out.

What are your strengths?

I am a pretty chill dog. I also do goofy things like running into table legs when chasing a toy. Some people think I'm funny on purpose.

What are your weaknesses?

Some people say I'm lazy. If I'm tired when someone calls me, I don't pay attention, I don't lift my head, and I can barely muster the energy to roll my eyes toward whoever calls me. The only time I say grumpy things to my family is when they try to make me get up while I'm snoozing and comfy.

What is your most memorable moment?

I'm smart enough to be sneaky, so nobody but me knows how many memorable moments I enjoyed. I had a lot of them, all in my favorite chair. I never get on the furniture with my family around, but when they go to bed, I get on the tan chair in the living room and sleep on my back with all four legs sticking up, chasing rabbits in my dreams. One night when I was in a deep sleep, I got caught. My family and I had to work through some trust issues after that.

Name: Bear
Breed: white German shepherd
How did you get to the farm?
I'm a very large dog (ninety pounds), and I was living in town at a house with a yard the size of a postage stamp. My owners there loved me but recognized my need for space and gave me to the Goggins. I was a little over a year old.
What are your strengths?
I am an impressive guard dog, and I'm the smartest dog the Goggins have ever had.
What are your weaknesses?
When I got to the farm, I was over-stimulated by all that was going on. I got a taste of freedom and went a little crazy. One day I was in the kitchen looking out the window when I saw something outdoors that interested me. I jumped through the screen window. I had to work on impulse control.
What is your most memorable moment?
Once I chased a deer across a long field and into the woods. I was as fast as the deer, but when shots rang out, I came home as quickly as I had left. Someone who was deer hunting at the time saw the whole race and told Mark about it. The thrill of the chase gets bigger when it's a deer instead of a squirrel. Only a few dogs would understand that.

Name: Rosie

Breed: white German shepherd

How did you get to the farm?

The Goggins purchased me from a puppy mill that looked a lot better on the internet than it looked in real life. I was sick for two months after they got me.

What are your strengths?

I'm really good at Frisbee. It's more than a game to me; I take Frisbee very seriously. Also, I am much more perceptive of what could happen than my friend Levi is.

What are your weaknesses?

My intelligence makes me psycho. Barometric pressure torments me, and I am terrified of storms. I don't just guard my people; I feel compelled to watch over the farm. Since I figured out Jason and Christina live just down the road, I have to guard their place too, from a distance. Relaxation is not a part of my life.

What is your most memorable moment?

Being chased by a deer, but that's another chapter, and I'm on duty, so I don't have time for this chitchat.

Name: Levi

Breed: part black Labrador, part husky, part Irish wolfhound. I have a silver beard, and my Civil War look alike is confederate General Jubal Early. I am a dog version of him.

How did you get to the farm?

I was raised on a farm in Ohio. I had a great upbringing, but my owner had to move to an apartment in town, and she didn't think I would be happy there. She put me on Craigslist in hopes of finding a good home for me. The Goggins saw my picture but decided to come and meet me despite my looks. They purchased me for thirty dollars, the best money they ever spent. I was four years old at the time.

What are your strengths?

I am a companion dog. While Rosie looks after the property, I look after my people. If they go to a different room, I do too. Although I am not the smartest dog that ever lived on this farm, I am most cooperative and train-able. I have a large repertoire of tricks, including sitting up on my hind legs.

What are your weaknesses?

When my family is gone and I am in the house alone, sometimes the kitchen wastebasket gets knocked over and trash gets strewn across the floor. When they get home, I refuse to go into the kitchen. People speculate that it's because I have a guilty conscience.

What is your most memorable moment?

One winter we had a lot of snow and school was can-celled for several days in a row. Annette was sitting at home bored when she remembered that my mother was a husky. She thought snow, a sled, and a part-husky dog sounded fun. At first it freaked me out a little bit, but I discovered I love to pull. Later, she bought a dog cart and trained Rosie and me to pull it. When Annette gets the dog cart out, I leap across the yard and then stand very still so that I can get my harness on. Children love riding in it. The dog cart experience is a strange mix of Amish and redneck. It's just good clean fun for all.

DEER

In March of 2016, Mark and I figured out we were running a game preserve and didn't even know it. We got a call from Christina. She and Jason had been driving past our house when they saw a natural phenomenon that caused them to stop and stare: Twenty-four deer had come out of our woods and were running toward the road. They (Jason and Christina, not the deer) called us and told us to look out the kitchen windows. We saw the deer too, but the dogs had barked at that point, so they were running away.

Our brave farm dogs, Levi and Rosie, started to chase them, but then Rosie (who is more cautious than Levi) counted the deer, saw that she and Levi were greatly outnumbered, and decided not to get involved. She told Levi to back off, and they headed home. Rosie had been through an unfortunate deer encounter before and seemed to be applying the lesson she had learned.

Rosie got her schooling one day when Mark and I and the two dogs had gone to the woods for a pleasant outing. I'm glad Mark was with me to testify to what happened that day, or I would have thought I was losing my mind. We were in the Ranger (an all-terrain vehicle), and both dogs were riding in the back. As we drove around in the woods, our white German Shepherd (Rosie) jumped out and went running. That was okay; the dogs always come home.

As we finished our little tour and approached the lane to drive back to the house, Mark stopped the Ranger so that I could help Levi get out of the back so that he could run. When I got out and walked to the back, I saw Rosie racing toward me. It was opposite day; instead of Rosie chasing a deer, a deer was chasing her!

In my previous deer experiences, the deer were timid and ran away from dogs or people. This deer, however, was on a tear, and it wasn't slowing down. It was running toward me now! I ran back around to the front of the Ranger, jumped in, and said, "Mark, a deer is chasing me!" She stopped about twenty feet from us, began walking toward us again, and then stood within fifteen feet for what seemed like a long time.

She must have been singing "If You're Happy and You Know It," in her mind, but she had changed it to "If You're Angry and You Know It." She was on the "stomp your feet" verse. She stood near us and stomped her front feet while we all—two dogs and two humans—watched, dumbfounded.

Levi, who was still in the back of the Ranger, was the first one to gather his wits. He remembered that he could bark, and his deep threat changed everything. The chase started again, this time with Levi and Rosie pursuing the deer. Levi didn't need any help getting out of the back end of the Ranger, and Rosie had a lot more confidence with Levi running ahead of her.

Levi's actions were almost as remarkable as the rest of the story. Mark yelled for him just one time, and he spun around in the middle of the field and came back as quickly as he had left to chase the deer. A dog that obeys immediately instead of following instinct is a pretty good dog. Not bad for a mutt we found on Craigslist for thirty dollars.

Rosie, meanwhile, followed Levi back. She had mud and dirt marks in several places on her white coat. Mark thinks the deer was protecting a fawn and had kicked or tried to stomp Rosie.

Deer look alike to me, so I can't be sure, but I think that same deer ventured near our yard at dusk on many evenings that summer. The dogs would go out and watch her while she watched them. She didn't seem to be afraid of them, and she even let Mark get close to her a time or two. Maybe it was her way of saying she had put the incident behind her.

4-H PIGS

We were a 4-H family, but barely: We were a fringe 4-H family, mainly only showing up for the fair. We went into high gear for 4-H a few days before the fair when the projects needed to be done.

Christina had some success in the photography category, despite the fact that her interest waned after her first mini-4-H photography project was judged. We left the project at the fairground on the due date and came back the next morning to see what the judges had decided. Making a beeline to her collage, we found that, oh joy, her project had a blue ribbon attached to the top corner! That joy began to fade as we looked around to see that every other child had also been awarded a blue ribbon.

Even a fourth grader knows the difference between being a winner and a participant. Either that or Lake Woebegone isn't the only place where all of the children are above average.

Gus had a stint in shooting sports. That only lasted a year, but his skills came in handy when we needed to kill varmints on the farm, particularly the possum who lied to us about his physical condition. We believed the possum until we found his "corpse" much closer to the house than the spot where he had originally expired.

Our strong suit was the 4-H swine club. The kids showed pigs for several years. Showing a 4-H pig involves getting in a sawdust-floored ring with a dozen or so other youngsters and walking around with the pig. A pig isn't led with a rope as a cow or horse can be, nor does it take to commands such as "heel," as man's best friend does.

Showing a pig means the pig gets to go where it pleases and the human taps (or hits) the pig with a short, stout stick if the pig tries to squeeze through a partly-opened gate or if there is some kind of pig altercation in the ring.

If a 4-H pig stops to "root" in the sawdusty manure on the floor of the arena, a vigorous tap will follow. The pig (and perhaps its owner) has been scrubbed down and powdered up extensively for this occasion. This is no time for porcine behavior.

Showing swine worked out well for our family. I even showed a pig in the open swine show at the Indiana State Fair. My husband talked me into it, and I agreed, envisioning myself much like one of the wholesome farm folk in *Charlotte's Web*. We unloaded the pig, and Mark stayed beside me as we worked our way through the maze of fences and gates that led to the arena.

Pigs and their owners were lined up, waiting to be allowed to enter. The whole setup was a warped version of waiting to get on a ride at Disney World. The good news is that I didn't have to ride a roller coaster with a pig when we got to the front of the line. The bad news is that Mark eventually left me to go get a seat in the bleachers.

At that point I realized I was a stranger to the whole situation. I had never spent any significant time with any pig in my life, including this one. We had barely been introduced, and now Farmer Mark was gone. I made an awkward attempt at establishing some kind of a friendship with the pig, but alas, the gates were opened and all of the porkers and their people were suddenly herded into the arena.

I concentrated intently on keeping track of my pig. They all looked the same to me now, pinkish-tan with floppy ears. My main concern was staying with the pig I came with, an idea that can be applied with wisdom to many situations in life.

My pig and I survived our moments of glory, and Mark found us at the exit chute. It was my first and last trip to the show ring.

SWINE CLUB

The 4-H swine club met once each month. In order to show pigs at the fair, a 4-Her had to attend at least one regular meeting of the swine club. As "fringe" 4-Hers, our kids only attended one meeting yearly. By the time the kids got into middle school, the thrill of showing a pig had been replaced by other pursuits: church activities, academics, sports, and theatre.

When the time came around and Mark told the kids they had to go to the 4-H meeting, he was met with some resistance. Gus didn't mind too much. He was a kid who found a way to be happy in almost any situation; he made it a goal to make others happy as well.

This was an endearing quality to most people, but not to his math teacher. They did not see the world on coordinate planes.

Attending the swine club meeting was a very unwelcome prospect to Christina. By middle school she was already in the habit of making lists, prioritizing, and budgeting time. The swine club meeting was not in her budget. Further, the whole swine scene was becoming less and less appealing to a farm girl who went to school with town kids. So, as the three of them—Mark, Gus, and Christina—left for the meeting, one of them was very grumpy.

They arrived at the meeting as misfits among the regular attenders, some of whom made the swine club their life's number one priority. The meeting they had chosen to attend turned out to be extra long because the club was electing officers for next year.

First, they elected a president. That was an obvious call, even to outsiders. A boy named Daniel was nominated and elected with no competition. If swine had been a subject of study in school, Daniel would have been the valedictorian. If passion for pigs could be transferred into money in a (piggy) bank, Daniel would have been a millionaire. He accepted his election with zeal: sultan of swine, president of pork, head honcho of hogs.

Next, a vice president had to be elected. Larry, the adult in charge of the swine club, asked for nominations. Nobody presented a name. The silence became awkward, but an idea was forming in Gus's mind. He was a little bit put out with his sister for various reasons. One, she was his older sister, which is explanation enough. Two, she sometimes put a damper on his carefree, fun-filled worldview. Three, she had been particularly grumpy on the way to the club meeting. A beautiful picture of revenge formed in his head, and his hand went up.

"I'd like to nominate my sister, Christina."

And that's how Christina became the vice president of the swine club for a year. When she left the house, she was grumpy. When she came back from the meeting as the new vice president, she looked like she'd been killing snakes. Unlike the president, Daniel, she did not carry the title with pride.

If the whole debacle has any redeeming value, her stint as an officer did look good on her scholarship applications. Gus would point out that she has him to thank for that.

NEW NEIGHBORS

My husband has lived within the same square mile for most of sixty years. The house we live in is the house he grew up in. He's at home here. His grandfather farmed this land, and his father farmed this land. Farmers don't pass a baton, but Mark has the hay hook now. When I ask Mark for directions, I get details like, "Go past where the viaduct used to be and turn right," or "Turn left at the old Garber place," although a Garber hasn't lived there for twenty years.

Our nearest neighbors are the Leemans, and they farm the ground next to ours. One day as we drove past the Leeman farm, Mark was talking about doing something with Barney Millis, whom we also consider a neighbor, even though he lives a couple of miles down the road and around the corner another half mile.

I was curious and asked, "You seem to be better friends with Barney than you are with the Leemans, even though the Leemans live closer. Why is that?"

Mark thought about it for a minute and said, "Well, I guess it's because Barney has been my neighbor for a long time."

That answer momentarily satisfied me, but one more question popped into my head after I had thought about it. "How long have you been neighbors with the Leemans?"

"Only twenty-five years."

RADISHES AND GAS

Mark and I don't care about radishes. I hardly ever take radishes when I eat at a salad bar, but this year Mark planted thirty-five acres of them in a field by our house and forty-five acres in a field down the road across from where Christina and Jason live. He isn't going to harvest them. They are simply a cover crop that helps break up the soil. Mark planted the radishes in July after he took the winter wheat and straw off the field. These radishes are called oilseed radishes, and they look more like carrots than radishes, except that they are as big around as a baseball bat and are nearly two feet long.

Since this is the first year Mark has planted radishes, it's been interesting. We were told that they would smell really bad as they began to rot in the field; we warned our neighbors to expect that well in advance.

We didn't expect the crop to be so intriguing to people driving down the road. The radishes were odd because they not only grew down into the ground, but also peeped their white tops out above the ground. Friends would stop me in the hall at school to say, "We drove past your farm the other day. What does Mark have planted in those fields?"

From our house, we have watched people stop their cars and get out to look at the plants. Strangers stopped at our house to ask about them. One old man in overalls came to our door and asked if he could pull up some radishes so that his family could cook the greens.

Mark said, "Help yourself; I have a lot of them."

Fast forward six months. One snowy Sunday night in late January, I was home trying to stay warm while Mark was at church for the yearly business meeting. Christina called to ask something about teaching, and as we were about to hang up, she said, "You know about the drama down here, don't you?"

"No, what are you talking about?" I asked.

"A volunteer fireman came to the door to tell me they are looking for a natural gas leak. There are four fire trucks outside our house, and swarms of firemen in our yard and the field beside us."

"Why do they think there is a gas leak?" I asked her.

Christina explained that a state policeman had stopped a guy for speeding near their house, and when he got out of the car, he had noticed a strong smell of gas and called the fire department. After the fireman told her this story, she told him that she and Jason had smelled it off and on for several days, but thought maybe it was a dead animal that had been hit by a car and was rotting in a ditch somewhere nearby.

While Christina was talking to me on the phone, I opened our door and sniffed outside. With the wind coming from the direction of her house, I could smell it too, and I was very concerned. In our part of Indiana, natural gas explosions have taken out entire blocks of downtown stores (in Richmond) and have turned peaceful fields into infernos that defied firefighters (near Sulphur Springs).

Christina and Jason's house has a natural gas line running into it, and so does our house. I had visions of our houses exploding but hardly knew where to tell her to go for safety. I did what I usually do when I don't know what to do. I said, "I need to call your dad," and hung up.

I called Mark and began to tell him what I knew. When he could get a word in edgewise, he said, "I know. I am down here with the firemen. I was on my way home from church when I saw the lights and came down to see what's going on."

"What are they doing now?"

"They're looking for a gas leak. I'm going to stay down here for a while to see what we can figure out." I hung up the phone and said a prayer for everyone's safety. I'm pretty sure God chuckled.

Looking out the window toward Christina and Jason's house, I could see the flashing lights on the trucks and the flashlights of firefighters as they looked for the gas leak in the darkness. I have never been inside the mind of a firefighter, especially not one looking for a gas leak in the dark with a flashlight. The idea confounds me. What would a gas leak look like?

The situation reminded me of Thurber's story "The Night the Ghost Got In," except that we had firemen looking for gas instead of policemen looking for ghosts. Also, in Thurber's story, Grandpa, who had been sleeping in the attic, got confused and shot a gun, grazing a policeman.

In our case, Grandpa was in Florida, not the attic, so he wasn't there to shoot anyone.

After an hour or so of searching, Mark and the firemen gave up on the natural gas mystery. Someone suggested that the smell was stronger when the wind gusted from the southeast, giving rise to the theory that perhaps an LP gas tank was leaking in the Lannerd housing addition about a mile southeast of us across the fields as the crow flies.

January in Indiana is no time to linger outside, so the men said their goodbyes and went home. That night as we said our prayers, Mark and I again prayed for safety for ourselves and our neighbors, and we were able to sleep peacefully.

On my way home from school Monday, I was thinking about the awful gas leak. As I neared home and rounded the bend where the radish field starts, a terrible smell and a hilarious thought both hit me at the same time.

I called Mark and said, "It's the radishes! That's what the smell is." He was skeptical. I reminded him that we had been warned about how bad they would smell as they rotted. Still, he doubted. I told him I would Google it when I got home.

At the very same moment, Christina was driving home from teaching at her school, coming toward our farm from the other direction. As she drove past the radish field near her house, she looked over at the radishes and thought about how nice it was that what we had been told about them wasn't true; they really didn't smell that bad. That's when she put it together and called her dad, who couldn't answer because he was talking to me.

By the time she got to talk to him, I was in the house Googling "What do rotting radishes smell like?" I got the information I needed from the titles and first lines that came up. The mystery was solved, the danger was past, and we could all take a deep, stinky breath and relax.

Someone had to tell the fire department. I let Mark make that call.

MARKETING MATTERS

For my fiftieth birthday, I wanted a reel mower, a push mower, a vintage mower. I got one. It was red, it was new, it was sleek, and it was over for me halfway through the yard the first time I used it.

The mower spent four years in the garage, and I was dogged by guilt every time I saw it. Each summer I made myself mow with it at least once to do penance for buying the annoying thing. After four years of the guilt, I knew it was time to move past my bad decision. I took a picture of the mower and posted it on my Facebook page, along with the following ad:

> I am selling this Mascot Silent Cut 18 Deluxe Reel Mower for reasons that should be obvious already, but will soon become obvious to the lucky buyer. The mower hasn't been used much at all, but I felt like it took six years every time I mowed with it.

I don't have a place for it in my garage or my life. Only contact me if you love the environment more than you love yourself. I just checked the price on the internet. I can do much better at $100. Despite my lack of marketing finesse, I do want to sell it.

Several people posted humorous remarks, but nobody wanted to buy the mower. Who's surprised by that?

The week before Mother's Day, a great idea hit me. I loaded up the mower and drove down the road to my favorite greenhouse, Fisher's, which is owned by an Amish family. I pulled up next to the building, opened the hatch on the Prius, showed Mr. Fisher the mower, and offered to make a trade. Twenty minutes later, my car was full of fragrance and one hundred dollars' worth of flowers.

As I pulled out of the driveway, one of the Fisher girls was mowing the lawn with my trade in. Sometimes things work out.

AFTERWORD

"Our Father refreshes us on the journey with some pleasant inns, will not encourage us to mistake them for home. We were made for another world."

C. S. Lewis

This book isn't the whole truth, nor is it the whole story. The schoolhouse, church house, and farmhouse are pleasant inns. Home will be even better.

NOTES

GetSub Grief

Now that we have been using GetSub for a few years, teachers are hardly ever asked to cover a class during their preparation hour if another teacher is absent. The problem is resolved in other ways.

Pregnant

Thank you to Luther Prater for letting me use your email.

Heaven

The lyrics to "O Think of the Home Over There" were written by DeWitt C. Huntington. Tullius C. O'Kane put them to music.

"When I Get to the End of the Way" was written by Charles Davis Tillman in 1885.

Farmhouse

Local legend says that James Whitcomb Riley was a friend of the Ellabargers and visited them, quoting poetry in what is now our living room.

Dogs

Charles Dickens wrote "It was the best of times, it was the worst of times" in *A Tale of Two Cities*.

4-H Pigs

To read more about Lake Wobegone, read *Lake Wobegone Days* by Garrison Keillor.

Charlotte's Web is by E.B. White.

Afterword

Lewis, C. S., *The Problem of Pain*. New York, NY: HarperOne, 2001. Print.

CONTACT INFORMATION

To order additional copies of this book, please visit
www.redemption-press.com.
Also available on Amazon.com and BarnesandNoble.com
Or by calling toll free 1-844-2REDEEM.